The Big Book of
Little Quilts

51 Patterns, Small in Size, Big on Style

Martingale
Create with Confidence

The Big Book of Little Quilts: 51 Patterns, Small in Size,
Big on Style
© 2019 by Martingale & Company

Martingale®
19021 120th Ave. NE, Ste. 102
Bothell, WA 98011-9511 USA
ShopMartingale.com

Printed in China
24 23 22 21 20 19   8 7 6 5 4 3 2 1

Library of Congress Cataloging-in-Publication Data is
available upon request.

ISBN: 978-1-68356-011-1

MISSION STATEMENT

We empower makers who use fabric and yarn
to make life more enjoyable.

CREDITS

**PUBLISHER AND
CHIEF VISIONARY OFFICER**
Jennifer Erbe Keltner

CONTENT DIRECTOR
Karen Costello Soltys

PRODUCTION MANAGER
Regina Girard

MANAGING EDITOR
Tina Cook

**COVER AND
BOOK DESIGNER**
Kathy Kotomaimoce

COPY EDITOR
Melissa Bryan

PHOTOGRAPHER
Brent Kane

DESIGN MANAGER
Adrienne Smitke

Contents

INTRODUCTION   5

FRESH TAKES

Double Dutch	7
Kitchen Corner	9
Sunrise	13
Bitty Churn Dash	19
Garden Bed	21
Spools	27
Stars and Stripes	31
Color Fusion	35
Cabin Skein	39
Tranquility	43
Quarter Log Cabin	47
Willow Tree Lane	51
Starburst	57
Mini Charm Star	65
Teatime	69

RETRO FAVES

Bayside	73
Dainty Dishes	77
Tilly's Basket Sampler	79
Little Strippy	91
Dixie	95
Tic-Tac-Toe	99
Windowpane	103
Susan's Courage	107
Opposition	111
Redware and Harvest	115
Bonnet Ties	119
Joyful Jumble	123
President's Pride	125
Courthouse Steps	131
Allie Beane	135

APPLIQUÉ

June Bug	139
Forever Friends	143
Parkersburg	147
Strawberry Fields Bird	153
Beach Ball Pinwheels	159
Feels Like Home	163
Game Day	169
Star Flowers and Berries	173
Bird Family	179
Oak Patch	183
Bedford Reels	189
Dresden Candy Dish	195
Friendship Star	199

HOLIDAY

Hanging Around	203
Birdsong	207
Merry Christmas to All	211
Seeing Stars	217
Heart and Home	221
Portraits of Santa	227
Tiny Trees	233
Little Snowman	237

Introduction

What kind of quilt offers huge opportunities? A little one, of course! A small quilt satisfies a host of needs. Want to whip up a quick gift, break open a fabric bundle, brighten a spot on the wall? A little quilt is the answer. Ready to luxuriate in making—and finishing—a quilt in a reasonable amount of time? Little quilts are here for you. Eager to whittle down the scrap pile or affordably indulge in beautiful new fabric? Little quilts, all the way.

To make it easy to find the type of little quilt you're looking for, we've organized the patterns in this book into sections. "Fresh Takes" suit current design trends and feature innovative patterns, "Retro Faves" honor tradition and mingle gorgeous reproduction fabrics, "Appliqué" beauties sprinkle their surfaces with both traditional motifs and delightful surprises, and "Holiday" designs are ready to enhance your decor or become heartfelt gifts.

Whether you want to stitch in brief chunks of time or dedicate a single blissful afternoon to your sewing machine, a little quilt is the itty-bitty jewel waiting to reward your effort. You'll have a finished quilt in no time and find that, with a little quilt, you can make very big memories indeed.

Happy sewing!

~The Editors at Martingale

Double Dutch

The Four Patch, with alternating light and dark fabric squares, offers easy piecing and a simple, timeless quilt to be enjoyed for generations. The size of Double Dutch makes it perfect to go everywhere with a new baby and to be long loved by a toddler.

Finished quilt: 36½" × 36½"
Finished block: 4" × 4"

*Designed and quilted by Amy Ellis;
pieced by Shelly Pagliai*

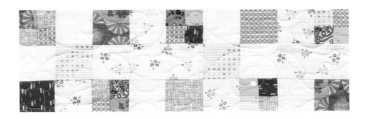

Materials

Yardage is based on 42"-wide fabric.

1¼ yards *total* of assorted light prints for blocks
¾ yard *total* of assorted medium prints for blocks
⅜ yard of fabric for binding
1¼ yards of fabric for backing
42" × 42" piece of batting

Cutting

All measurements include ¼"-wide seam allowances.

From the assorted light prints, cut a *total* of:
41 matching pairs of 1 square, 2½" × 2½", and
     1 rectangle, 2½" × 4½"
80 squares, 2½" × 2½"

From the assorted medium prints, cut a *total* of:
80 squares, 2½" × 2½"
164 squares, 1½" × 1½"

From the binding fabric, cut:
4 strips, 2¼" × 42"

One at a Time

For each of the Four Patch blocks, you'll need the following:
     2 light 2½" squares
     2 medium 2½" squares

For each of the Framed Four Patch blocks, you'll need the following:
     4 medium 1½" squares
     1 light 2½" square and 1 matching
     2½" × 4½" rectangle

Making the Four Patch Blocks

Press all seam allowances as indicated by the arrows or as otherwise specified.

1 Sew each medium 2½" square to a light 2½" square. Make 80 pairs.

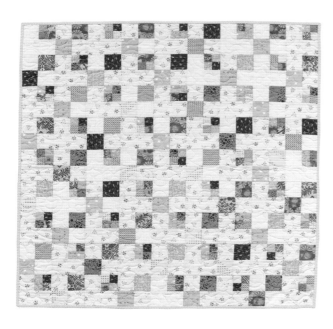

4 Join a matching light 2½" × 4½" rectangle to the top of each unit from step 3 to make a total of 41 Framed Four Patch blocks.

Make 41.

Assembling the Quilt Top

1 Lay out nine rows of nine blocks each, alternating the blocks as shown.

2 Sew the blocks together into rows, pressing the seam allowances in alternate directions from row to row. Sew the rows together to complete the quilt top. Press the seam allowances in one direction.

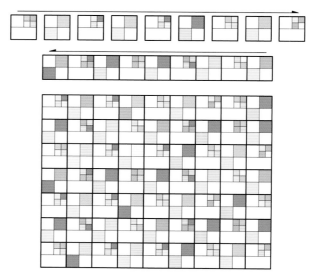

Quilt assembly

2 Nesting the seams, sew together two of the units made in step 1. Make 40 Four Patch blocks.

Make 40.

Making the Framed Four Patch Blocks

1 Sew the medium 1½" squares together into 82 pairs.

2 Nesting the seams, join the units from step 1 into pairs to make 41 small Four Patch blocks.

Make 41.

3 Join each small Four Patch block to one side of a light 2½" square.

Finishing the Quilt

For help with the following finishing steps, go to ShopMartingale.com/HowtoQuilt for free, illustrated instructions.

1 Layer and baste the quilt top, batting, and backing. Quilt by hand or machine.

2 Using the 2¼"-wide strips of binding fabric, prepare and attach double-fold binding. Add a hanging sleeve, if desired.

4 *The Big Book of Little Quilts*

Kitchen Corner

A small project is a fun way to play with color and fabrics while making something new to decorate your space. To give your quilt some depth and add interest, choose scrappy fabrics in varying shades and prints within each color family.

Finished quilt: 36½" × 36½"
Finished block: 6" × 6"

Designed and made by Amy Smart

Materials

Yardage is based on 42"-wide fabric.

36 squares, 6¼" × 6¼", of assorted pink, gold, and blue prints for blocks
½ yard of cream print for blocks
⅜ yard of gold stripe for binding
1⅛ yards of fabric for backing
40" × 40" piece of batting

Cutting

All measurements include ¼"-wide seam allowances.

Print squares:
Cut each 6¼" square in half diagonally to yield 72 triangles.

From the cream print, cut:
9 strips, 1½" × 42"; crosscut into 36 rectangles, 1½" × 10"

From the gold stripe, cut:
2½"-wide bias strips totaling at least 154" when joined

Straighten Up

If you're using a diagonal stripe or prefer a straight-grain binding, cut four crosswise strips, 2½" × 42", from the gold stripe.

Making the Blocks

For each block, choose two contrasting triangles and one 1½" × 10" cream rectangle. Press all seam allowances as indicated by the arrows.

1 Fold the triangles and rectangle in half to find their centerlines and finger-press. Sew the long edge of a triangle to one long edge of the cream rectangle, matching the centers. Repeat to sew a

Assembling the Quilt Top

1 Arrange the blocks in six rows of six blocks each, rotating the blocks as shown to create a lattice pattern.

2 Sew the blocks together into rows, and then join the rows.

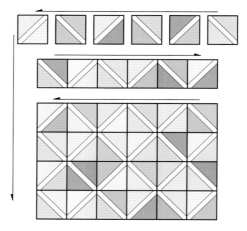

Quilt assembly

contrasting triangle to the opposite edge of the same cream rectangle. Make 36 blocks.

Make 36.

2 Trim each block to measure 6½" square, keeping the cream rectangles centered.

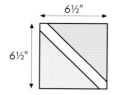

6½"

6½"

Finishing the Quilt

For help with the following finishing steps, go to ShopMartingale.com/HowtoQuilt for free, illustrated instructions.

1 Layer and baste the quilt top, batting, and backing. Quilt by hand or machine. The quilt shown is machine stitched in the ditch along the horizontal and vertical block grid, with diagonal lines echoing the cream rectangles.

2 Using the gold stripe 2½"-wide bias strips, prepare and attach double-fold binding.

3 Add a hanging sleeve, if desired.

Sunrise

Greet each day with a smile! Whether it's sunny outside or not, Sunrise is sure to brighten your outlook. And, with paper-foundation piecing, you'll be able to stitch perfect points on the sun rays, giving you another reason to smile.

Finished quilt: 28½" × 35½"
Finished block: 7" × 7"

Designed and made by Kate Henderson

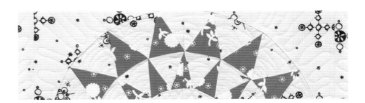

Materials

Yardage is based on 42"-wide fabric. Fat quarters are 18" × 21"; fat eighths are 9" × 21".

2¾ yards of white print for background
8 fat quarters of assorted orange prints for blocks
4 fat eighths of assorted orange prints for blocks
⅜ yard of orange print for binding
1⅜ yards of fabric for backing
35" × 42" piece of batting
Template plastic
Paper for foundation piecing

Cutting

All measurements include ¼"-wide seam allowances. Trace patterns A, B, and E on page 16 onto template plastic and cut them out. Use the templates to cut the pieces from the fabrics indicated below.

From the white print, cut:
10 strips, 3¼" × 42"; crosscut into 100 rectangles,
    3¼" × 3¾"
7 strips, 2¾" × 42"; crosscut into 80 rectangles,
    2¾" × 3¼"
20 of piece B
20 of piece E

From *each* orange print fat quarter, cut:
2 strips, 2¾" × 21"; crosscut into 10 rectangles,
    2¼" × 2¾" (80 total)
2 strips, 3¼" × 21"; crosscut into 8 rectangles,
    2¾" × 3¼" (64 total)
2 of piece A (16 total)

From *each* orange print fat eighth, cut:
1 strip, 2¾" × 21"; crosscut into 5 rectangles,
    2¼" × 2¾" (20 total)
1 strip, 3¼" × 21"; crosscut into 4 rectangles,
    2¾" × 3¼" (16 total)
1 of piece A (4 total)

From the orange print for binding, cut:
4 strips, 2½" × 42"

Piecing the Foundation Units

For more details on paper-foundation piecing, go to ShopMartingale.com/HowtoQuilt for free downloadable information. Press all seam allowances toward each newly added piece as you go.

1 Using the patterns on page 17, make 20 copies each of units C and D, being sure to copy the patterns at 100%. Roughly cut out each pattern, leaving ¼" of paper all around the dashed outer lines. Reduce the stitch length on your sewing machine to 1.5 mm, or about 17 to 18 stitches per inch.

4 Pin a white 3¼" × 3¾" rectangle on top of the orange piece, right sides together. Flip the unit over, paper side up, and sew on the line between areas 2 and 3. Open the white rectangle and make sure it covers area 3. Press. Fold *only* the paper on the line between areas 3 and 4; trim the excess fabric so that it extends ¼" beyond the fold.

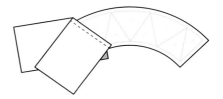

5 Continue adding white 3¼" × 3¾" rectangles and matching orange 2¾" × 3¼" rectangles in the same way until unit D is completely covered with fabric. Use a rotary cutter to trim the paper and fabrics on the dashed outer line. Carefully remove the paper. Make a total of 20 D units.

Unit D.
Make 20.

6 Repeat steps 2–5 using pattern C, orange 2¼" × 2¾" rectangles, and white 2¾" × 3¼" rectangles. Each unit begins and ends with an orange rectangle. Make a total of 20 C units.

Unit C.
Make 20.

Making the Blocks

Press all seam allowances as indicated by the arrows.

1 Lay out one orange A piece, one white B piece, one C unit, one D unit, and one white E piece; all the orange pieces should match. Fold each piece in half and finger-press to mark the centers. Pin the B piece on top of the A piece, right sides together, matching the center and easing the fabric to fit. Sew the pieces together.

2 Place a white 3¼" × 3¾" rectangle on the wrong side of a D pattern, covering area 1. Place an orange 2¾" × 3¼" rectangle on top of the white rectangle, right sides together. Make sure the fabrics extend at least ¼" beyond the stitching lines. Pin in place. Flip the unit over, paper side up, and sew on the line between areas 1 and 2.

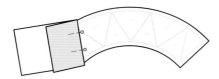

3 Open the orange rectangle and make sure it covers area 2. Press. Fold *only* the paper on the line between areas 2 and 3; trim the excess fabric so that it extends ¼" beyond the fold. Unfold the paper and make sure both fabrics are right side up.

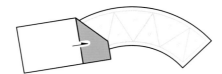

2 Repeat step 1 to sew the C unit, D unit, and E piece to complete one block. Make a total of 20 blocks measuring 7½" square, including seam allowances.

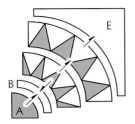

Make 20 blocks, 7½" × 7½".

Assembling the Quilt Top

1 Arrange the blocks in five rows of four blocks each, making sure to place blocks with matching orange fabrics next to each other as shown in the quilt assembly diagram below. Sew the blocks together into rows. Join the rows to complete the quilt top. The quilt top should measure 28½" × 35½".

2 Stitch around the perimeter of the quilt top, ⅛" from the outer edges, to lock the seams in place.

Finishing the Quilt

For help with the following finishing steps, go to ShopMartingale.com/HowtoQuilt for free, illustrated instructions.

1 Layer and baste the quilt top, batting, and backing. Quilt by hand or machine. The quilt shown is free-motion quilted in each shaped piece with a variety of different motifs, including swirls, spirals, and pebbles.

2 Using the orange 2½"-wide strips, prepare and attach double-fold binding.

3 Add a hanging sleeve, if desired.

Quilt assembly

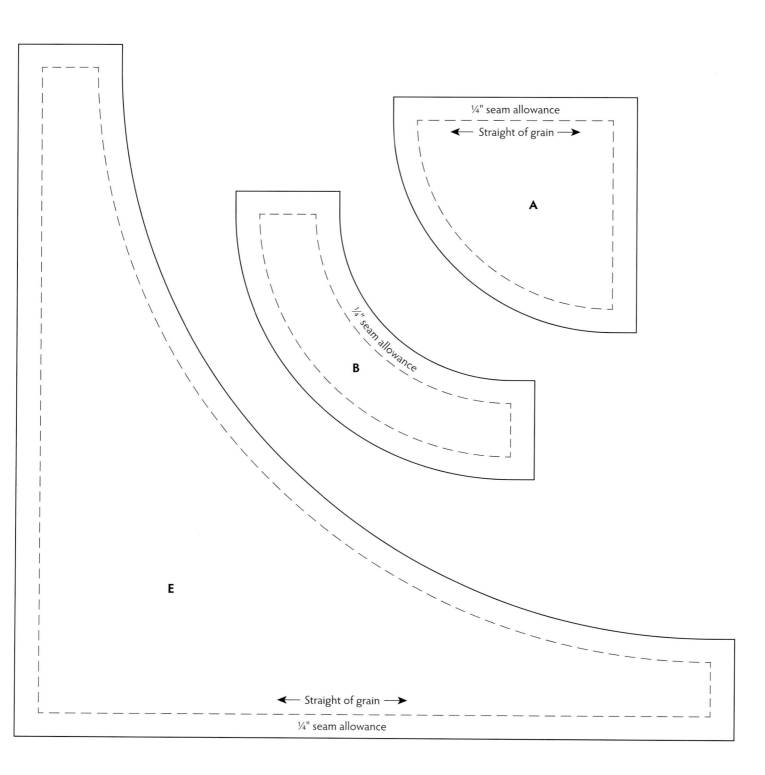

¼" seam allowance

← Straight of grain →

A

¼" seam allowance

B

E

← Straight of grain →

¼" seam allowance

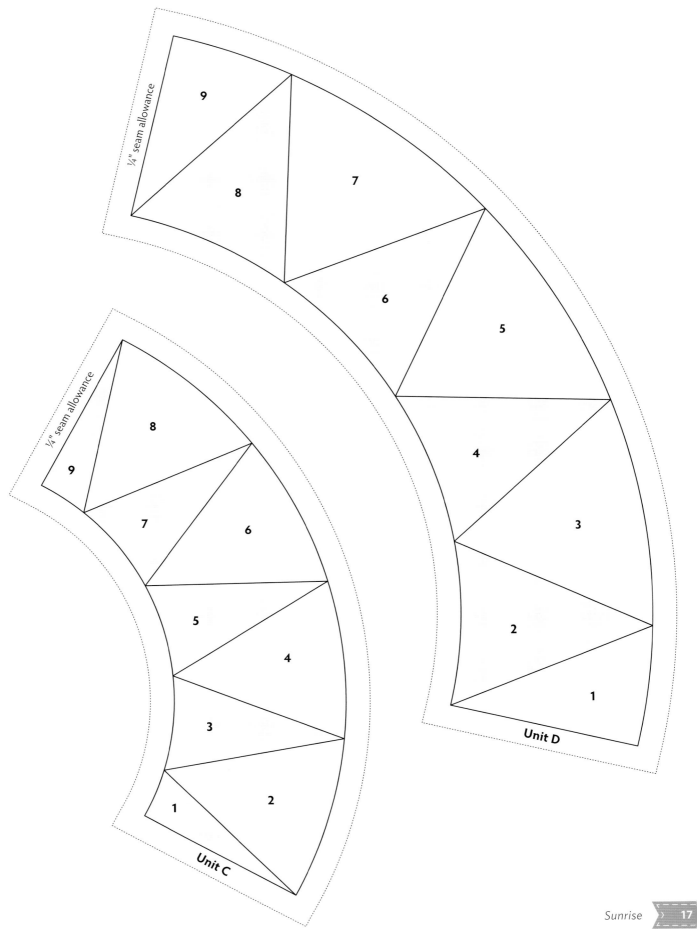

¼" seam allowance

9

8

7

6

5

4

3

2

1

Unit D

¼" seam allowance

8

9

7

6

5

4

3

2

1

Unit C

Bitty Churn Dash

Time to celebrate color! Splash your brightest fabrics across a backdrop of black-and-white prints for a cheerful take on the classic Churn Dash. Subtle gray cornerstones keep things interesting without overpowering the design.

Finished quilt: 16¾" × 21"
Finished block: 3½" × 3½"

Designed and made by Mary Etherington and Connie Tesene

Materials

Yardage is based on 42"-wide fabric.

½ yard *total* of assorted bright scraps for blocks
½ yard *total* of assorted light scraps for blocks
¼ yard of white solid for sashing strips
⅛ yard of gray print for cornerstones
¼ yard of beige print for binding
¾ yard of fabric for backing
25" × 29" piece of batting

Cutting

All measurements include ¼"-wide seam allowances.

From assorted bright scraps, cut 20 matching sets of:
2 squares, 2⅜" × 2⅜"; cut in half diagonally to yield
    4 triangles (20 sets of 4 triangles, 80 total)
4 squares, 1" × 1" (80 total)

From assorted light scraps, cut 20 matching sets of:
2 squares, 2⅜" × 2⅜"; cut in half diagonally to yield
    4 triangles (20 sets of 4 triangles, 80 total)
1 square, 1" × 1" (20 total)
4 rectangles, 1" × 1½" (80 total)

From the white solid, cut:
1 strip, 4" × 42"; crosscut into 31 rectangles, 1¼" × 4"

From the gray print, cut:
1 strip, 1¼" × 42"; crosscut into 12 squares, 1¼" × 1¼"

From the beige print, cut:
2 strips, 2¼" × 42"

Making the Blocks

Each block uses four light triangles, one light 1" square, and four light 1" × 1½" rectangles—all matching—as well as four matching bright triangles and four matching bright 1" squares. Press all seam allowances as indicated by the arrows.

1   Sew a light triangle to a bright triangle on the diagonal, being careful not to stretch the bias edges. The half-square-triangle unit should measure 2" square, including seam allowances. Make four units using the same light and bright fabrics.

Make 4.

2   Sew a light rectangle to a bright square. Make four units that measure 1" × 2", including seam allowances.

Make 4.

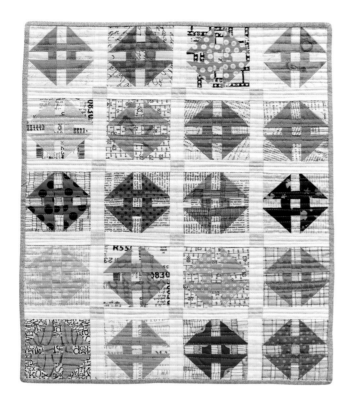

Assembling the Quilt Top

1 Arrange the blocks, white sashing rectangles, and gray cornerstones in horizontal rows as shown below.

2 Sew the pieces together into rows, and then join the rows.

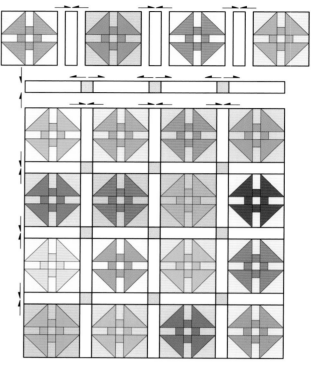

Quilt assembly

3 Arrange the units from steps 1 and 2 and a matching light 1" square in three horizontal rows. Sew the pieces together into rows and then join the rows. The block should measure 4" square, including seam allowances. Make 20 Churn Dash blocks.

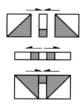

Make 20.

Keeping Rows Straight

Adding cornerstones to your sashing is an easy way to make sure each row aligns with the other rows.

Finishing the Quilt

For help with the following finishing steps, go to ShopMartingale.com/HowtoQuilt for free, illustrated instructions.

1 Layer and baste the quilt top, batting, and backing. Quilt by hand or machine. The quilt shown is machine quilted with closely spaced parallel horizontal lines known as matchstick quilting.

2 Using the beige 2¼"-wide strips, prepare and attach double-fold binding.

3 Add a hanging sleeve, if desired.

Garden Bed

Charming pink daisies (or are they coneflowers?) and blue forget-me-nots adorn the edges of this easy-to-piece table topper. Gail chose variegated floss colors to add a bit of additional whimsy to the embroidery.

Finished quilt:
32½" × 32½"

Designed and made by Gail Pan

Materials

Yardage is based on 42"-wide fabric unless noted otherwise. Fat eighths are 9"×21".

⅜ yard of beige tone on tone for embroidery backgrounds

1 fat eighth *each* of 2 blue, 3 green, and 3 red prints for squares

½ yard of small-scale blue print for squares and binding

½ yard of red print for borders

1¼ yards of fabric for backing

37" × 37" piece of batting

1⅓ yards of lightweight fusible interfacing, 18" to 20" wide, for embroidery backings

6-strand variegated embroidery floss in pine green, moss green, mint green, light pink, dark red, and blue

Size 8 pearl cotton in ecru

¼" quilter's tape (optional)

Cutting

All measurements include ¼"-wide seam allowances.

From the beige tone on tone, cut:
2 strips, 5" × 42"; crosscut into 4 strips, 5" × 21"

From the lightweight fusible interfacing, cut:
4 strips, 5" × 21"

From *1* of the blue fat eighths, cut:
1 square, 4½" × 4½"
4 squares, 3½" × 3½"

From *each of 2* of the green fat eighths, cut:
1 square, 4½" × 4½" (2 total)
4 squares, 3½" × 3½" (8 total)

From *each of the 5* remaining fat eighths, cut:
4 squares, 3½" × 3½" (20 total)

From the small-scale blue print, cut:
4 strips, 2½" × 42"
1 square, 4½" × 4½"
4 squares, 3½" × 3½"

From the red print for borders, cut:
2 strips, 1½" × 42"; crosscut into:
- 2 strips, 1½" × 20½"
- 2 strips, 1½" × 18½"
4 strips, 2½" × 42"; crosscut into:
- 2 strips, 2½" × 32½"
- 2 strips, 2½" × 28½"

swirl flower only once, even if they don't overlap exactly; their alignment doesn't need to be perfect. Fuse the interfacing strips to the wrong side of the marked strips.

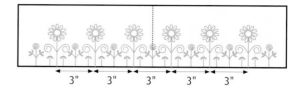

3 Using two strands of floss, embroider the designs following the stitch key and color guides on the pattern.

Assembling the Quilt Top

Press all seam allowances as indicated by the arrows or as otherwise specified.

1 Centering the embroidery, trim the embroidered border strips to 4½" × 20½".

2 Lay out the 3½" squares in six rows of six squares each, as shown below. Sew the squares together into rows. Press the seam allowances in opposite directions from row to row. Sew the rows together to complete the quilt center; press the seam allowances in one direction.

3 Sew the red 1½" × 18½" strips to the sides of the quilt. Sew the red 1½" × 20½" strips to the top and bottom of the quilt.

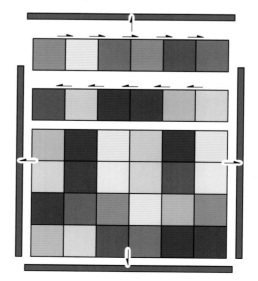

Embroidering the Border Strips

For help with basic hand-embroidery stitches, go to ShopMartingale.com/HowtoQuilt for free downloadable information.

1 Finger-press a beige tone-on-tone 5" × 21" strip in half widthwise to create a center fold. Open the strip and draw a small line in the bottom *seam allowance*, 1½" to the right of the fold. Measure 3" to the right of this line and draw another line as before. Draw a third line, 3" to the right of the last one. These lines indicate where to place the large daisy flower stems. Repeat on the left side of the strip, beginning 1½" to the left of the fold. Mark all four of the beige 21"-long strips in this manner.

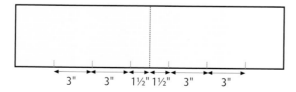

2 Using the pattern on page 25, trace the Garden Bed design onto the right side of the marked strips, lining up the daisy stem in the design with the small marked lines in the seam allowance. Trace each

5 Sew the red 2½" × 28½" strips to the sides of the quilt. Sew the red 2½" × 32½" strips to the top and bottom of the quilt.

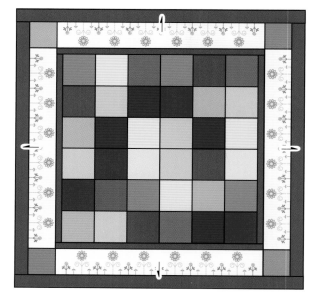

Quilt assembly

4 Sew embroidered strips to the sides of the quilt, making sure the stems are oriented toward the quilt edges. Sew a green 4½" square to the left end of each remaining embroidered strip and a blue 4½" square to the right end of each remaining embroidered strip. Making sure the stems are oriented toward the quilt edges, stitch the pieced border strips to the top and bottom of the quilt.

Finishing the Quilt

For help with the following finishing steps, go to ShopMartingale.com/HowtoQuilt for free, illustrated instructions.

1 Layer and baste the quilt top, batting, and backing. Quilt by hand or machine. In the quilt shown, pearl cotton and big-stitch quilting create an X in each center and border square. With ¼" quilter's tape used as a guide, quilting is added ¼" from the seamline in all of the red border strips.

2 Using the blue print 2½"-wide strips, prepare and attach double-fold binding before completing the quilting next to the binding seam.

3 Add a hanging sleeve, if desired.

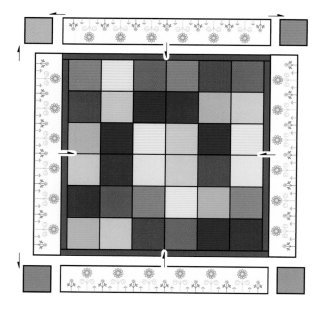

Embroidery Key

◯ Lazy daisy

• French knot

⊓⊓⊓ Blanket stitch

— Backstitch

Blanket stitch

Garden Bed Table Mat

Spools

Sew, flip, repeat! Adorable Spool blocks are not only fun to make, but also use up lots of scraps! This variation of a traditional Spool or Bow Tie block uses one print for each spool, except for one scrappy block. The background fabric is the same throughout.

Finished quilt: 36½" × 36½"
Finished block: 6" × 6"

Designed and made by Pat Sloan

Materials

Yardage is based on 42"-wide fabric.

½ yard *total* of assorted pink and red prints for blocks and pieced border
½ yard *total* of assorted aqua prints for blocks and pieced border
½ yard of pink-with-white dot for blocks, inner border, and pieced border
¾ yard of white solid for blocks and pieced border
⅜ yard of red dot for binding
1⅓ yards of fabric for backing
42" × 42" piece of batting

Cutting

All measurements include ¼"-wide seam allowances.

From the assorted pink and red prints, cut a *total* of:
7 rectangles, 2½" × 6½"
64 squares, 2½" × 2½"

From the assorted aqua prints, cut a *total* of:
8 rectangles, 2½" × 6½"
64 squares, 2½" × 2½"

From the pink-with-white dot, cut:
2 strips, 2½" × 28½"
2 strips, 2½" × 24½"
1 rectangle, 2½" × 6½"
4 squares, 2½" × 2½"

From the white solid, cut:
2 strips, 6½" × 42"; crosscut into 32 rectangles, 2½" × 6½"
4 strips, 2½" × 42"; crosscut into 64 squares, 2½" × 2½"

From the red dot, cut:
4 strips, 2¼" × 42"

Making the Blocks

Press all seam allowances as indicated by the arrows.

1 Draw a diagonal line from corner to corner on the wrong side of four matching pink or red squares. Place a marked square on one end of a white rectangle, right sides together. Sew on the drawn line. Trim ¼" from the stitching line, and press toward the resulting pink triangle. Repeat on the other end of the rectangle to make a side unit. Make two matching units measuring 2½" × 6½", including seam allowances.

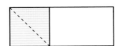
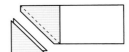

Make 2.

Making the Pieced Border

1 Lay out eight aqua squares, six pink/red squares, and 14 white squares in two rows as shown. Join the squares in each row. Join the rows to make the left side border.

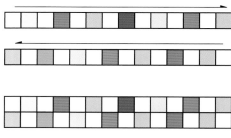

Left side border

2 Repeat step 1 using seven aqua squares, seven pink/red squares, and 14 white squares to make the right side border.

Right side border

3 In the same way, use nine pink/red squares, nine aqua squares, and 18 white squares to make the top border. Repeat to make the bottom border.

Top border

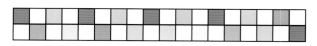

Bottom border

Assembling the Quilt Top

1 Lay out the blocks in four rows of four blocks each, alternating the pink/red blocks and the aqua blocks as shown in the quilt assembly diagram on page 29.

2 Sew the blocks together into rows, and then join the rows.

2 Lay out the side units and one matching pink or red rectangle as shown. Join the pieces to make a block. In the same way, make a total of eight pink (or red) blocks.

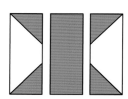 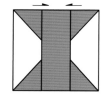

Make 8.

3 Repeat steps 1 and 2 using aqua squares and rectangles to make eight blocks.

Make 8.

3 Sew the pink-and-white 24½"-long strips to the top and bottom of the quilt top. Sew the pink-and-white 28½"-long strips to the sides of the quilt top to complete the inner border.

4 Sew the left and right pieced borders to the quilt top. Sew the top and bottom pieced borders to the quilt top.

Finishing the Quilt

For help with the following finishing steps, go to ShopMartingale.com/HowtoQuilt for free, illustrated instructions.

1 Layer and baste the quilt top, batting, and backing. Quilt by hand or machine. The quilt shown is machine quilted with an interlocking design in the center. The inner border is left unquilted, and a repeating triangle design is added to the pieced outer border.

2 Using the red dot 2¼"-wide strips, prepare and attach double-fold binding.

3 Add a hanging sleeve, if desired.

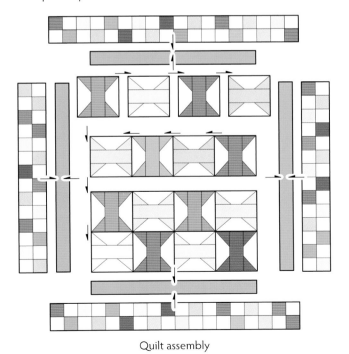

Quilt assembly

Stars and Stripes

Martha Washington was not only a strong, patriotic woman but is also considered the mother of our country. The Star blocks in this sweet little table topper bear her name. This star-studded quilt is easily put together in a weekend.

Finished quilt: 14" × 18½"
Finished block: 4½" × 4½"

Designed and made by Kathy Flowers

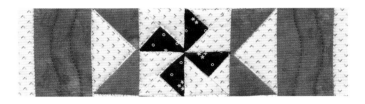

Materials

Yardage is based on 42"-wide fabric. Fat quarters are 18" × 21".

½ yard of cream print for blocks and border
½ yard of blue print for blocks, border, and binding
¼ yard of red print for blocks and border
1 fat quarter of fabric for backing
18" × 21" piece of batting

Cutting

All measurements include ¼"-wide seam allowances.

From the cream print, cut:
1 strip, 3½" × 42"; crosscut into 2 squares, 3½" × 3½".
    Cut into quarters diagonally to yield 8 C triangles.
1 strip, 2⅜" × 42"; crosscut into 4 squares, 2⅜" × 2⅜".
    Cut into quarters diagonally to yield 16 A triangles.
1 strip, 2" × 42"; crosscut into 8 squares, 2" × 2". Cut in
    half diagonally to yield 16 B triangles.
1 strip, 2" × 42"; crosscut into 2 strips, 2" × 18½"
1 strip, 1⅝" × 42"; crosscut into 8 squares, 1⅝" × 1⅝"

From the blue print, cut:
1 strip, 3½" × 42"; crosscut into 2 squares, 3½" × 3½".
    Cut into quarters diagonally to yield 8 C triangles.
1 strip, 2⅜" × 42"; crosscut into 4 squares, 2⅜" × 2⅜".
    Cut into quarters diagonally to yield 16 A triangles.
1 strip, 2" × 42"; crosscut into 2 strips, 2" × 18½"
1 strip, 1⅝" × 42"; crosscut into 8 squares, 1⅝" × 1⅝"
2 strips, 2½" × 42"

From the red print, cut:
1 strip, 2" × 42"; crosscut into 16 squares, 2" × 2". Cut
    in half diagonally to yield 32 B triangles.
1 strip, 2" × 42"; crosscut into 2 strips, 2" × 18½"

Making the Blocks

Press all seam allowances as indicated by the arrows.

1 Align one cream A triangle atop one blue A triangle, right sides together. Join along one short edge to make a blue-and-cream triangle unit. Repeat to make a total of 16 blue-and-cream triangle units, always placing the blue triangle on the bottom.

4 Sew two red B triangles to one blue C triangle as shown to make a flying-geese unit. Repeat to make a total of eight red-and-blue flying-geese units. Using 16 red B triangles and eight cream C triangles, repeat to make a total of eight red-and-cream flying-geese units.

Make 8 red and blue.
Make 8 red and cream.

5 Sew two red-and-blue flying-geese units to opposite edges of one Windmill block.

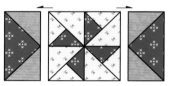

6 Sew blue 1⅝" squares to opposite ends of two red-and-blue flying-geese units.

Make 2.

7 Sew the flying-geese units from step 6 to the top and bottom edges of the Windmill block to make a red-and-blue Martha Washington Star block. Repeat to make a second red-and-blue Martha Washington Star block.

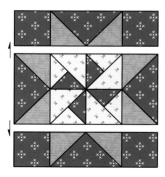

Make 2.

2 Align one cream B triangle with one blue-and-cream triangle unit. Sew along the long edge to make a windmill unit. Repeat to make a total of 16 windmill units.

Make 16.

3 Lay out four windmill units as shown; sew together in pairs. Join the windmill-unit pairs as shown to make a Windmill block. Repeat to make a total of four Windmill blocks.

Make 4.

The Big Book of Little Quilts

8　Using the remaining Windmill blocks, the red-and-cream flying-geese units, and the cream 1⅝" squares, repeat steps 5–7 to make two red-and-cream Martha Washington Star blocks.

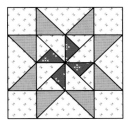

Make 2.

9　Sew the four blocks together, alternating the dark and light blocks to make the quilt center.

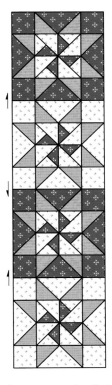

10　Sew together one each of the red, cream, and blue 2" × 18½" strips along the long edges to make a border unit as shown. Repeat to make a second border unit.

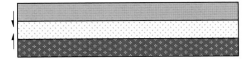

Make 2.

11　Match the center of one border unit with the quilt center along one long edge; pin. Sew the border unit to the quilt center. Repeat to add the remaining border unit to the remaining long edge of the quilt center to complete the quilt top.

Finishing the Quilt

For help with the following finishing steps, go to ShopMartingale.com/HowtoQuilt for free, illustrated instructions.

1　Layer and baste the quilt top, batting, and backing. Quilt by hand or machine. The quilt shown is machine quilted in the ditch in the blocks. Double wavy lines accent the red strips in the borders. A straight line is stitched down the center of each red and cream strip, and diamond shapes are stitched in each blue strip.

2　Using the blue 2½"-wide strips, prepare and attach double-fold binding.

3　Add a hanging sleeve, if desired.

Color Fusion

Color is one of the tools quilters work with every day. In addition to having fun making this fabric version of the color wheel, you'll find it to be a great accent piece whether displayed in your quilting studio, thrown over a chair, or used as a table topper.

Finished quilt: 38½" × 38½"

Designed and made by Natalie Barnes; quilted by Angela Walters

Materials

Yardage is based on 42"-wide fabric. Fat quarters are 18" × 21".

1 fat quarter *each* of red, yellow, blue, green, orange, violet, yellow-green, blue-green, blue-violet, red-violet, red-orange, and yellow-orange solids
1 fat quarter *each* of small-scale red, yellow, blue, green, orange, violet, yellow-green, blue-green, blue-violet, red-violet, red-orange, and yellow-orange prints
⅜ yard of gray solid for binding
1⅜ yards of fabric for backing
44" × 44" piece of batting
Creative Grids 30° Triangle ruler (CGRSG1)

Cutting

All measurements include ¼"-wide seam allowances.

From *each* of the solids, cut:
1 strip, 11½" × 21"; crosscut into:
- 1 rectangle, 11" × 11½" (12 total)
- 1 rectangle, 3" × 11½" (12 total)

From *each* of the small-scale prints, cut:
1 strip, 6½" × 21"; crosscut into 1 rectangle, 6½" × 11½" (12 total)

From the gray solid, cut:
4 strips, 2¼" × 42"

Making the Color Wedges

Press all seam allowances as indicated by the arrows.

1 On a flat surface, arrange the 12 solid 11" × 11½" rectangles and 12 print 6½" × 11½" rectangles in color-wheel order, beginning with red and referring to the diagram on page 37. Place each 3" × 11½" strip with its complementary color, the color that is opposite on the color wheel. For example, put the smaller green piece with the larger red piece. Continue until all of the complementary fabrics are paired with the solids and prints.

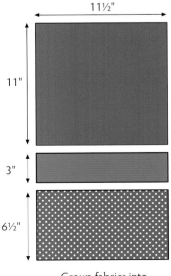

Group fabrics into 12 complementary sets.

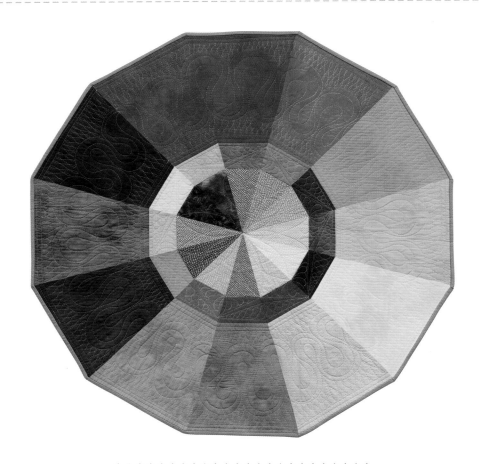

2 Sew the red solid 11" × 11½" rectangle, the green solid 3" × 11½" rectangle, and the red print 6½" × 11½" rectangle together as shown to form one piece that measures 11½" × 19½". Continue with the remaining colors, selecting the next set of three fabrics, and sew them together.

3 Place the narrow end of the 30° triangle ruler on the print fabric, aligned with the raw edge. The seams of the 2½" strip of complementary color should align with the lines on the ruler. Using your rotary cutter, cut on each side of the ruler to make one large 30° wedge, 19½" long. Repeat for each pieced unit from step 2 to cut 12 wedges.

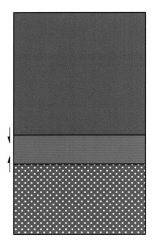

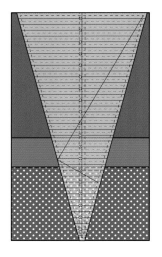

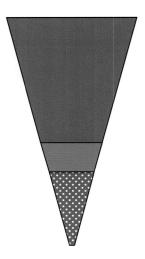

Assembling the Quilt Top

1 Place the wedges in color-wheel order again with red at the top. Pin the red and red-orange adjacent color-wheel wedges together, matching the 2½"-strip seams, and stitch them together. Sew the wedges together in sets of three to form four "blocks," red to orange, yellows, green to blue, and violets.

2 Sew two of the blocks together in color order. Join the remaining two in the same manner, pressing the seam allowances open. Finally, sew these two pieces together, taking care to sew slowly through the bulk in the center of your piece.

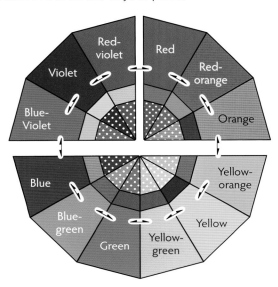

Finishing the Quilt

For help with the following finishing steps, go to ShopMartingale.com/HowtoQuilt for free, illustrated instructions.

1 Layer and baste the quilt top, batting, and backing. Quilt by hand or machine. The quilt shown is machine quilted with overlapping loops in the center wedges and a serpentine design in the outer wedges.

2 Using the gray 2¼"-wide strips, prepare and attach double-fold binding.

3 Add a hanging sleeve, if desired.

Cabin Skein

You may have heard of a gaggle of geese, but this quilt is named for a flock of geese in flight, also known as a skein. Delve into your scrap basket to make this showstopping quilt featuring small versions of classic Log Cabin blocks and flying-geese units.

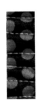

Finished quilt: 20½" × 20½"
Finished block: 4" × 4"

Designed and made by Carrie Nelson

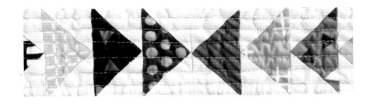

Materials

Yardage is based on 42"-wide fabric.

8 squares, 10" × 10", of assorted dark prints for blocks and sashing*
8 squares, 10" × 10", of assorted light prints for blocks and sashing*
¼ yard of gray homespun for binding
¾ yard of fabric for backing
23" × 23" piece of batting

Precut 10" squares work perfectly for this project. Use more than eight prints to achieve a scrappier look.

Cutting

All measurements include ¼"-wide seam allowances.

From the assorted dark prints, cut:
20 squares, 3¼" × 3¼"
16 squares, 1½" × 1½"
36 *lengthwise* strips, 1" × 10"; crosscut into:
- 16 rectangles, 1" × 4½"
- 16 rectangles, 1" × 4"
- 16 rectangles, 1" × 3½"
- 16 rectangles, 1" × 3"
- 16 rectangles, 1" × 2½"
- 16 rectangles, 1" × 2"

From the assorted light prints, cut:
64 squares, 1⅞" × 1⅞"
34 *lengthwise* strips, 1" × 10"; crosscut into:
- 16 rectangles, 1" × 4"
- 16 rectangles, 1" × 3½"
- 16 rectangles, 1" × 3"
- 16 rectangles, 1" × 2½"
- 16 rectangles, 1" × 2"
- 16 rectangles, 1" × 1½"

From the gray homespun, cut:
3 strips, 2¼" × 42"

Stop the Stretch

Cutting the rectangles for the Log Cabin blocks along the *lengthwise* grain prevents stretching and distortion as you sew them. This helps keep the seams accurate and the block tidy and square. To determine the lengthwise grain, gently stretch the 10" squares; the lengthwise grain will have little or no stretch and the crosswise grain will have more give.

Making the Log Cabin Blocks

Press all seam allowances toward the rectangle just added.

1 Sew one light 1" × 1½" rectangle to the bottom of a dark 1½" square.

2 Sew a light 1" × 2" rectangle to the left side of the square. Sew a dark 1" × 2" rectangle to the top edge. Sew a dark 1" × 2½" rectangle to the right side.

3 Continue rotating the unit and adding rectangles in size order, creating the light/dark pattern. Add two more rounds until the block is 4½" square, including seam allowances. Make 16 Log Cabin blocks.

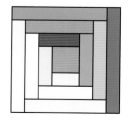

Make 16.

Making the Quarter-Square-Triangle Units

Press all seam allowances as indicated by the arrows.

1 Select four different dark 3¼" squares. Draw a diagonal line from corner to corner on the wrong side of two squares. Pair each marked square right sides together with an unmarked square. Sew a scant ¼" from both sides of the marked lines. Cut along the marked lines to yield four half-square-triangle units; press the seam allowances toward the darker fabric. Each half-square triangle should measure 2⅞" square, including seam allowances.

2 Draw a diagonal line perpendicular to the seam on the wrong side of one half-square-triangle unit. Place the marked unit right sides together with a second half-square-triangle unit, placing the seams perpendicular to each other. Sew a scant ¼" from both sides of the marked line. Cut along the line to yield two quarter-square-triangle units; press the seam allowances in one direction. Each unit should measure 2½" square. Make four quarter-square-triangle units for the sashing cornerstones.

Make 4.

Making the Flying-Geese Units

1 Draw a diagonal line from corner to corner on the wrong side of the light 1⅞" squares. Place two marked squares on opposite corners of one dark 3¼" square, right sides together as shown. Sew a scant ¼" from both sides of the drawn line.

2 Cut the unit along the drawn line to yield two units.

3 Place a marked light 1⅞" square with right sides together on the corner of each pressed unit, orienting the line as shown. Sew a scant ¼" from both sides of the line. Cut along the drawn line to yield two flying-geese units. Make 64 flying-geese units.

4 Lay out four flying-geese units in a row, pointing the same direction. Join the units. Make 16 flying-geese sashing rows. Each sashing row should measure 2½" × 4½", including seam allowances.

Make 16.

Assembling the Quilt Top

1 Arrange four Log Cabin blocks, four flying-geese rows, and one sashing cornerstone in three rows as shown. Orient the light side of the Log Cabin blocks to the outside edges. Sew the units together in each row, and then join the rows. Make four.

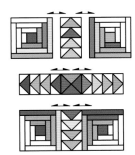

Make 4.

2 Lay out the units from step 1 in two rows of two. Sew together into rows, and then join the rows to complete the quilt top.

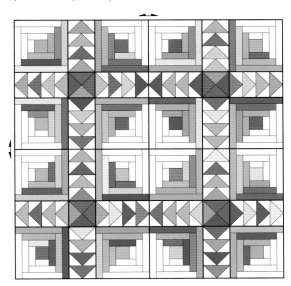

Quilt assembly

Finishing the Quilt

For help with the following finishing steps, go to ShopMartingale.com/HowtoQuilt for free, illustrated instructions.

1 Layer and baste the quilt top, batting, and backing. Quilt by hand or machine. The quilt shown is machine quilted with straight parallel lines, reminiscent of stacked logs.

2 Using the gray homespun 2¼"-wide strips, prepare and attach double-fold binding.

3 Add a hanging sleeve, if desired.

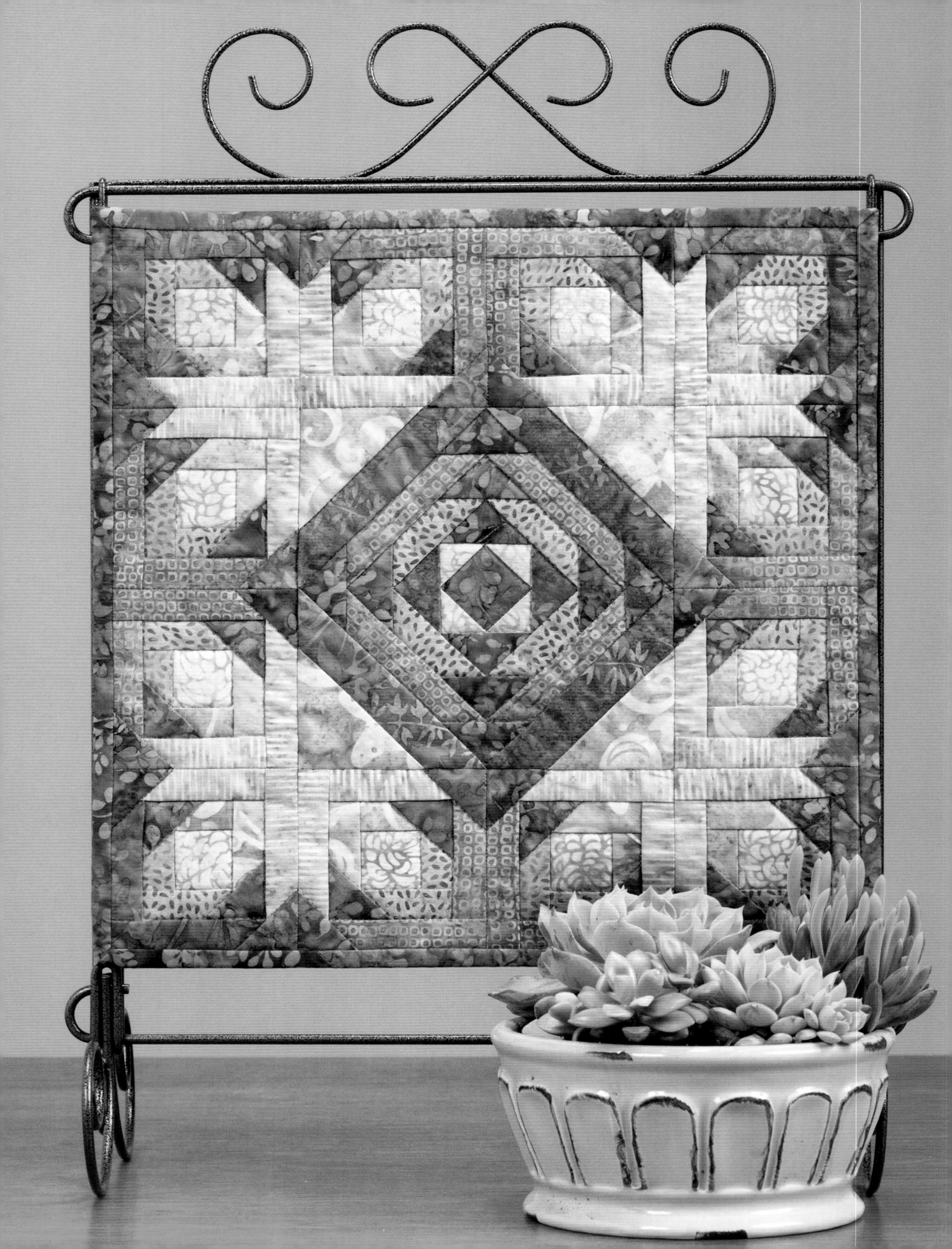

Tranquility

A soft blend of batik fabrics gives this quilt a peaceful feeling. Don't let the small pieces and points fool you—two easy-to-sew variations of Pineapple blocks are all this quilt requires. And the blocks are paper pieced for precision.

Finished quilt: 12½" × 12½"
Finished blocks: 6" × 6" and 3" × 3"

Designed and made by Connie Kauffman

Materials

Yardage is based on 42"-wide fabric.

⅛ yard *each* of medium blue #1, medium blue #2, light cranberry, medium cranberry, and dark cranberry batiks for blocks

⅛ yard of dark blue batik for blocks and single-fold binding

6" × 10" scrap of light blue batik for blocks

14" × 14" square of fabric for backing

14" × 14" square of batting

Paper for foundation piecing

Working with Batiks

Batiks are beautiful fabrics. One of their great qualities is that the print is the same on both the front and the back. This makes them very easy to use in paper piecing because you can place scraps any way they fit using either side of the fabric.

Cutting

Measurements include ¼"-wide seam allowances.

From the dark blue batik, cut:
2 strips, 1¼" × 42"

Making the Blocks

For more details on paper-foundation piecing, go to ShopMartingale.com/HowtoQuilt for free downloadable information.

1 Using the patterns on pages 45 and 46, make one copy of block A and 12 copies of block B/C.

2 Piece the A block using dark blue for pieces 1, 6–9, 14–17, and 22–25; light blue for pieces 2–5; light cranberry for pieces 10–13; medium cranberry for pieces 18–21; dark cranberry for pieces 26–29; and medium blue #2 for pieces 30–33.

3 Piece eight B blocks using light blue for piece 1; light cranberry for pieces 2 and 4; medium blue #2 for pieces 3 and 5; dark blue for pieces 6, 7, 12, and 13; medium cranberry for pieces 8 and 10; and medium blue #1 for pieces 9 and 11.

4 Piece four C blocks the same as block B, with one exception: for pieces 8 and 10, use dark cranberry rather than medium cranberry. These blocks with the darker fabric will form the corners of the quilt.

Block A.
Make 1.

Block B.
Make 8.

Block C.
Make 4.

Assembling the Quilt Top

Press all seam allowances open as indicated by the arrows.

1 Lay out the A, B, and C blocks in rows, rotating the B and C blocks as shown in the quilt assembly diagram at right. Join two B blocks to make a side row. Make two rows, and then sew them to opposite sides of block A. Join two B and two C blocks to make the top row. Repeat to make the bottom row. Sew these rows to the top and bottom of the A block to complete the quilt top, paying careful attention to the color placement.

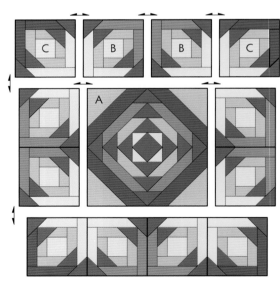

Quilt assembly

2 Remove the paper foundations. Press and trim the quilt top to measure 12½" square.

Finishing the Quilt

For help with the following finishing steps, go to ShopMartingale.com/HowtoQuilt for free, illustrated instructions.

1 Layer and baste the quilt top, batting, and backing. Quilt by hand or machine. The quilt shown is machine quilted in the ditch around all the squares and triangles.

2 Using the dark blue 1¼"-wide strips, prepare and attach single-fold binding (which some designers prefer to double-fold binding for small quilts).

3 Add a hanging sleeve, if desired.

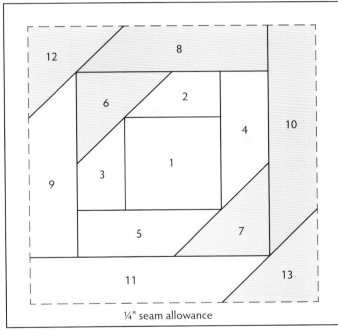

¼" seam allowance

Blocks B and C
Make 12.

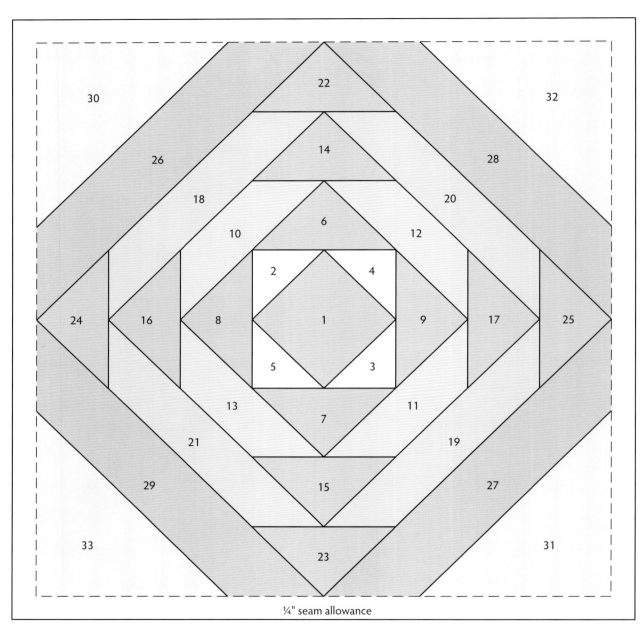

¼" seam allowance

Block A
Make 1.

Quarter Log Cabin

Many quilters want to make a baby quilt as their first project, and this is a nice candidate for a crib-size creation. You can also turn it into a beautiful lap quilt by adding borders, or by making more blocks using a variety of fabrics.

Finished quilt: 24½" × 24½"
Finished block: 12" × 12"

Designed and made by Pat Sloan

Materials

Yardage is based on 42"-wide fabric.

¼ yard of multicolored print (fabric A) for blocks
¼ yard of green print (fabric B) for blocks
⅜ yard of red floral (fabric C) for blocks
⅜ yard of orange print (fabric D) for blocks
⅜ yard of red print (fabric E) for binding
⅞ yard of fabric for backing
29" × 29" piece of batting

Cutting

All measurements include ¼"-wide seam allowances.

From the multicolored print (fabric A), cut:
4 squares, 6½" × 6½"

From the green print (fabric B), cut:
2 strips, 2½" × 42"; crosscut into:
- 4 strips, 2½" × 6½"
- 4 strips, 2½" × 10½"

From the red floral (fabric C), cut:
3 strips, 2½" × 42"; crosscut into:
- 4 strips, 2½" × 8½"
- 4 strips, 2½" × 10½"

From the orange print (fabric D), cut:
3 strips, 2½" × 42"; crosscut into:
- 4 strips, 2½" × 8½"
- 4 strips, 2½" × 12½"

From the red print (fabric E), cut:
3 strips, 2¼" × 42"

Making the Blocks

Press all seam allowances as indicated by the arrows.

1 Sew a 2½" × 6½" fabric B rectangle to a 6½" fabric A square. The unit should measure 6½" × 8½", including seam allowances. Sew a 2½" × 8½" fabric C rectangle to an adjacent side of the fabric A square. The unit should now measure 8½" square, including seam allowances. Make four units.

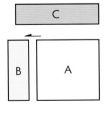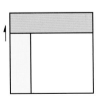

Make 4 units,
8½" x 8½".

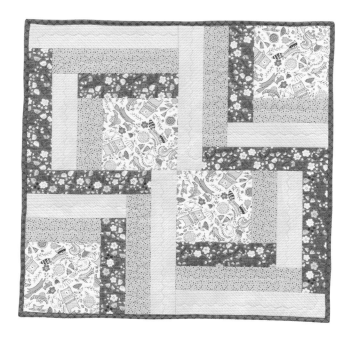

Assembling the Quilt Top

1. Lay out the blocks in two rows of two blocks each as shown in the quilt assembly diagram below.

2. Sew the blocks together into rows, and then join the rows.

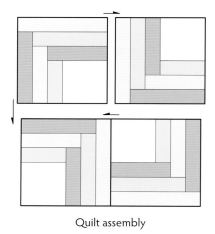

Quilt assembly

Finishing the Quilt

For help with the following finishing steps, go to ShopMartingale.com/HowtoQuilt for free, illustrated instructions.

1. Layer and baste the quilt top, batting, and backing. Quilt by hand or machine. The quilt shown is machine quilted with a wavy line through the middle of each round of rectangles on each block. A wavy line is also quilted diagonally through the center of each multicolored square.

2. Using the 2¼"-wide fabric E strips, prepare and attach double-fold binding.

3. Add a hanging sleeve, if desired.

2. Sew a 2½" × 8½" fabric D rectangle to a unit from step 1. Sew a 2½" × 10½" fabric B rectangle to the unit. The unit should measure 10½" square, including seam allowances. Make four units.

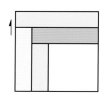
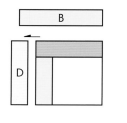

Make 4 units,
10½" x 10½".

3. Sew a 2½" × 10½" fabric C rectangle to a unit from step 2. Sew a 2½" × 12½" fabric D rectangle to the unit to complete a Quarter Log Cabin block. The block should measure 12½" square, including seam allowances. Make a total of four blocks.

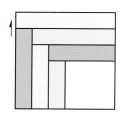
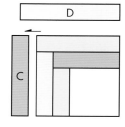

Make 4 blocks,
12½" x 12½".

Willow Tree Lane

Take a trip down a lane lined with whimsical houses and gorgeous willow trees. Snowball blocks provide the perfect frame for two charming embroidery scenes, while the pieced blocks and borders invite you to show off some of your coziest prints.

Finished quilt: 36½" × 36½"
Finished blocks: 6" × 6"

Designed and made by Gail Pan

Materials

Yardage is based on 42"-wide fabric unless otherwise noted.

½ yard of cream solid for embroidered blocks

⅜ yard of brown print for blocks

½ yard of red tone on tone for blocks

½ yard of red floral for blocks and outer border

⅝ yard of light green print for blocks and binding

¼ yard of brown dot for inner border

1¼ yards of fabric for backing

41" × 41" piece of batting

1⅛ yards of lightweight fusible interfacing, 18" to 20" wide, for embroidery backing

6-strand embroidery floss in brown, red, yellow, and variegated sage green

Size 8 pearl cotton in ecru

¼" quilter's tape (optional)

Cutting

All measurements include ¼"-wide seam allowances.

From the cream solid, cut:
2 strips, 7" × 42"; crosscut into 9 squares, 7" × 7"

From the lightweight fusible interfacing, cut:
9 squares, 7" × 7"

From the brown print, cut:
4 strips, 2½" × 42"; crosscut into 52 squares, 2½" × 2½"

From the red tone on tone, cut:
4 strips, 2½" × 42"; crosscut into:
- 16 strips, 2½" × 6½"
- 16 squares, 2½" × 2½"

From the red floral, cut:
2 strips, 2½" × 42"; crosscut into:
- 8 strips, 2½" × 6½"
- 8 squares, 2½" × 2½"
2 strips, 2½" × 32½"
2 strips, 2½" × 36½"

From the light green print, cut:
2 strips, 2½" × 42"; crosscut into:
- 8 strips, 2½" × 6½"
- 8 squares, 2½" × 2½"
4 strips, 2½" × 42"

From the brown dot, cut:
2 strips, 1½" × 30½"
2 strips, 1½" × 32½"

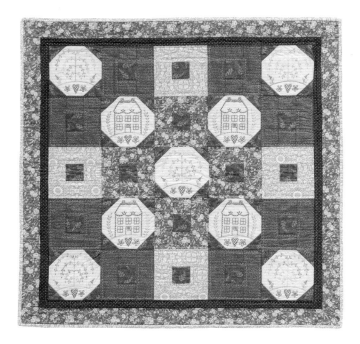

Embroidering the Designs

For help with basic hand-embroidery stitches, go to ShopMartingale.com/HowtoQuilt for free downloadable information.

1 Using the patterns on pages 54 and 55, trace the Tree design onto the right side of five of the cream squares and the House design onto the right side of the remaining four cream squares. Fuse an interfacing square to the wrong side of each of the marked squares.

2 Using two strands of floss, embroider the designs, following the stitch key and color guides on the patterns.

Making the Blocks

Press all seam allowances as indicated by the arrows or as otherwise specified.

1 Centering the embroidered design, trim the stitched squares to 6½" × 6½".

2 Mark a diagonal line from corner to corner on the *wrong* side of 36 brown 2½" squares. Aligning the corners, pin a marked square to an embroidered square, right sides together. Sew directly on the marked line. Trim ¼" outside the seamline and press. Repeat on all four corners of each embroidered square to make a total of nine embroidered Snowball blocks.

Make 9.

3 For each pieced block you'll need a set of two matching 2½" squares and two matching 2½" × 6½" strips, plus one brown 2½" square. Sew the matching squares to opposite sides of the brown square. Sew the matching strips to both long sides of the pieced strip to complete the block. Repeat to make eight red tone-on-tone blocks, four red floral blocks, and four light green blocks.

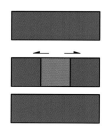 

Make 8.

Make 4 of each.

Assembling the Quilt Top

1 Lay out five rows of five blocks each, making sure all embroidered blocks are upright.

2 Sew the blocks together into rows, pressing the seam allowances open, and then join the rows.

3 Sew the brown-dot 30½"-long strips to opposite sides of the quilt top. Sew the brown-dot 32½"-long strips to the top and bottom of the quilt top.

4 Sew the red-floral 32½"-long strips to opposite sides of the quilt top. Sew the red-floral 36½"-long strips to the top and bottom of the quilt top.

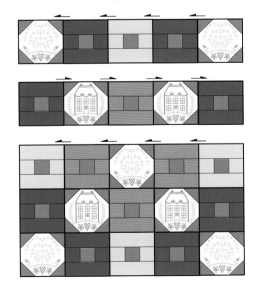

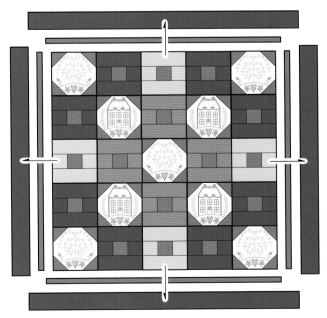

Quilt assembly

Finishing the Quilt

For help with the following finishing steps, go to ShopMartingale.com/HowtoQuilt for free, illustrated instructions.

1 Layer and baste the quilt top, batting, and backing. Quilt by hand or machine. In the quilt shown, pearl cotton and big-stitch quilting are used to quilt ¼" from the brown center square and ¼" from the seamline in each pieced block and in the borders.

2 Using the light green 2½"-wide strips, prepare and attach double-fold binding before completing the quilting next to the binding seam.

3 Add a hanging sleeve, if desired.

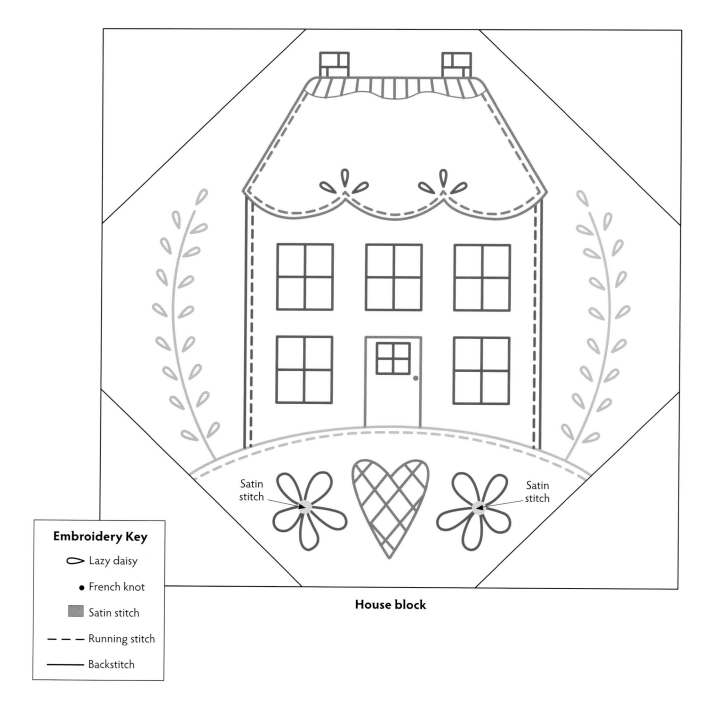

Satin stitch

Satin stitch

House block

Embroidery Key

⌒ Lazy daisy

● French knot

▨ Satin stitch

– – – Running stitch

——— Backstitch

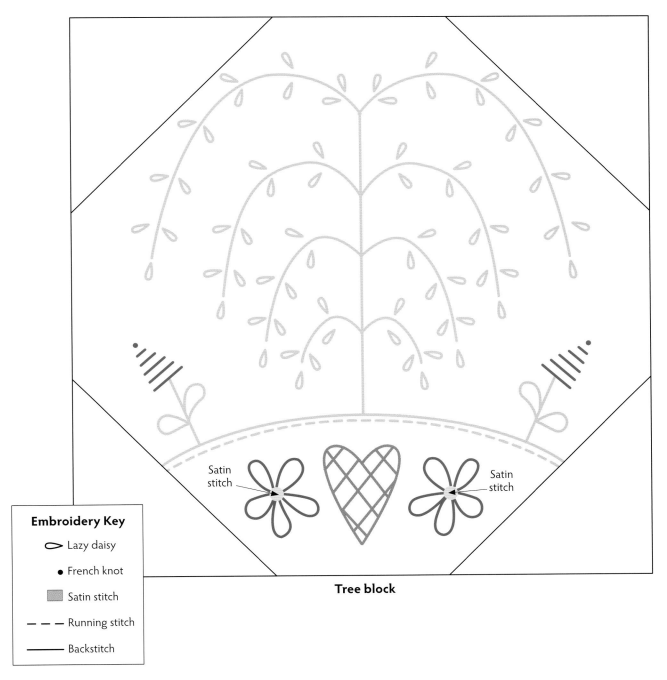

Embroidery Key

⬭ Lazy daisy

● French knot

▨ Satin stitch

– – – Running stitch

— Backstitch

Satin stitch

Satin stitch

Tree block

Starburst

This little paper-pieced gem is for those who like a challenge! Color selection is crucial, as subtle shading is employed to give the illusion of depth and movement. A single Starburst will shine on its own, but you can also group two or even four for a striking display.

Finished quilt:
12½" × 12½"

Designed and made by Connie Kauffman

Materials

Yardage is based on 42"-wide fabric.

¼ yard of black solid for blocks and single-fold binding
Scraps of batiks, solids, or mottled prints in the following colors for blocks: white, light red, light green, light yellow, light teal, light purple, light blue, light orange, medium red, medium green, medium yellow, medium teal, medium purple, medium blue, and medium orange
14" × 14" square of fabric for backing
14" × 14" square of batting
Paper for foundation piecing

Cutting

Measurements include ¼"-wide seam allowances.

From the black solid, cut:
2 strips, 1¼" × 42"

Making the Blocks

For more details on paper-foundation piecing, go to ShopMartingale.com/HowtoQuilt for free downloadable information.

Pay close attention to the pattern labels. In addition to patterns A–F, you'll need the reverse of A–E, which are labeled A reversed, B reversed, and so on. The lighter shade of each color is used in the reversed pattern. For example, you'll use medium yellow, medium orange, and so on in A, and light yellow, light orange, and so on in A reversed. Mark your patterns carefully.

1 Using the patterns on pages 61–64, make four copies *each* of units A and A reversed. Make one copy *each* of units B, B reversed, C, C reversed, D, D reversed, E, and E reversed.

2 Piece the units as follows:
Unit A: Use medium yellow for pieces 1 and 10; black for pieces 2, 5, and 9; medium orange for piece 3; medium blue for piece 4; white for piece 6; medium purple for piece 7; and medium teal for piece 8.

Unit A reversed: Use light yellow for pieces 1 and 10; black for pieces 2, 5, and 9; light orange for piece 3; light blue for piece 4; white for piece 6; light purple for piece 7; and light teal for piece 8.

Units B, C, D, and E: Use medium green for piece 1, black for pieces 2 and 5, medium red for piece 3, and white for piece 4.

Units B reversed, C reversed, D reversed, and E reversed: Use light green for piece 1, black for pieces 2 and 5, light red for piece 3, and white for piece 4.

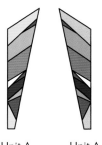

Unit A reversed.　　Unit A.

Make 4 of each.

Unit B reversed.　　Unit B.

Make 1 of each.

Trim as You Go

After sewing and pressing each seam, it's helpful to trim the excess fabric that extends beyond the paper. It may also be helpful to pin or glue the fabrics in place for sewing.

Unit C reversed.　　Unit C.

Make 1 of each.

Unit D reversed.　　Unit D.

Make 1 of each.

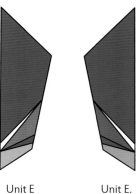

Unit E reversed.　　Unit E.

Make 1 of each.

Assembling the Quilt Top

Press all seam allowances open as indicated by the arrows or as otherwise specified.

1 Lay out the units in a fan shape with the fabric right side up as shown in the quilt layout at right. This will help keep the units in order and is a good way to double-check that you have all the lighter colors on one side and the darker colors on the other side.

2 Sew an A reversed unit to the B reversed unit using a ¼" seam allowance and offsetting the units as shown. (Or, you can pin through the points in each corner to make sure they're lined up correctly.)

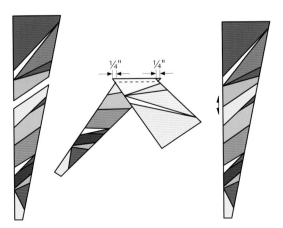

3 In the same way, join an A unit to the C unit. Join an A reversed unit to the D reversed unit. Join an A unit to the E unit. Join an A reversed unit to the E reversed unit. Join an A unit to the D unit. Join an A reversed unit to the C reversed unit. Join an A unit to the B unit. Press the seam allowances open.

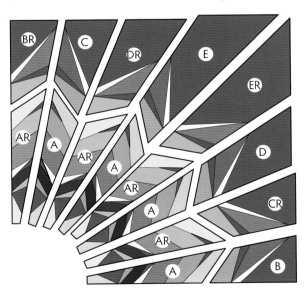

Quilt layout

4 Sew the units together, carefully matching the seam intersections.

Quilt assembly

5 Cut one light yellow F shape using the pattern on page 62. Turn under the curved edge ¼". Hand appliqué the shape to the corner of the unit from step 4 to complete the quilt top.

6 Remove the paper foundations. Press and trim the quilt top to measure 12½" square.

Finishing the Quilt

For help with the following finishing steps, go to ShopMartingale.com/HowtoQuilt for free, illustrated instructions.

1 Layer and baste the quilt top, batting, and backing. Quilt by hand or machine. The quilt shown is machine quilted in the ditch along most of the pieces in the colored rays. Curved lines are quilted in the center arc, and radiating lines are added in the outer black area.

2 Using the black 1¼"-wide strips, prepare and attach single-fold binding (which some designers prefer to double-fold binding for small quilts).

3 Add a hanging sleeve, if desired.

Enlarging Options

You can make two quilts of this design and rotate one of them 90° so that, when displayed side by side, they look like half a star or a sunrise. If you're even more ambitious, make four Starburst quilt tops and join them to create a complete star that measures 24" square.

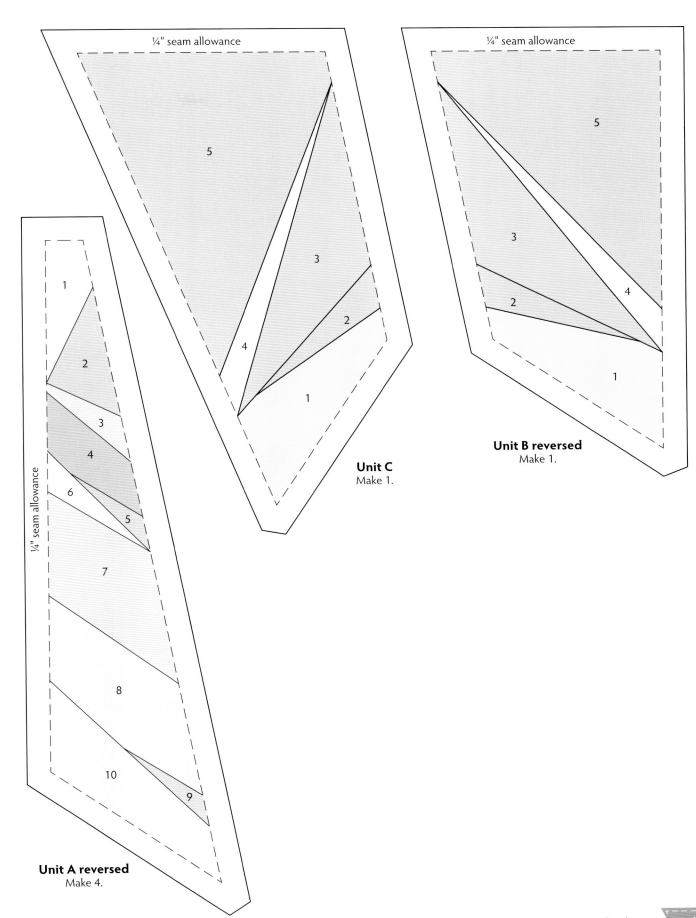

¼" seam allowance

5

3

4

2

1

Unit C
Make 1.

¼" seam allowance

5

3

2

4

1

Unit B reversed
Make 1.

¼" seam allowance

1

2

3

4

6

5

7

8

10

9

Unit A reversed
Make 4.

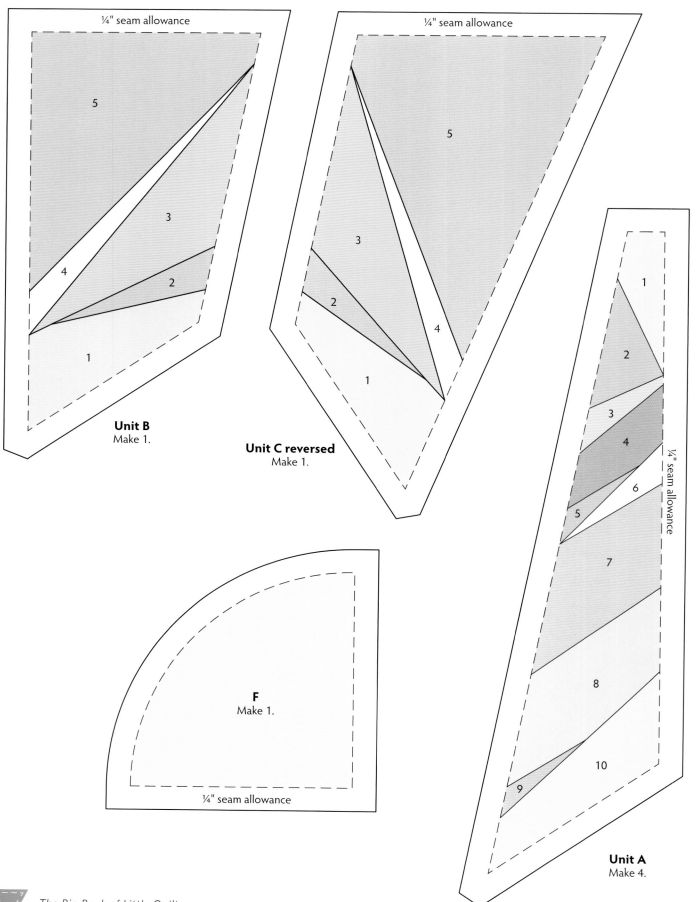

¼" seam allowance

5

3

4

2

1

Unit B
Make 1.

¼" seam allowance

5

3

2

4

1

Unit C reversed
Make 1.

1

2

3

4

6

5

¼" seam allowance

7

8

10

9

Unit A
Make 4.

F
Make 1.

¼" seam allowance

The Big Book of Little Quilts

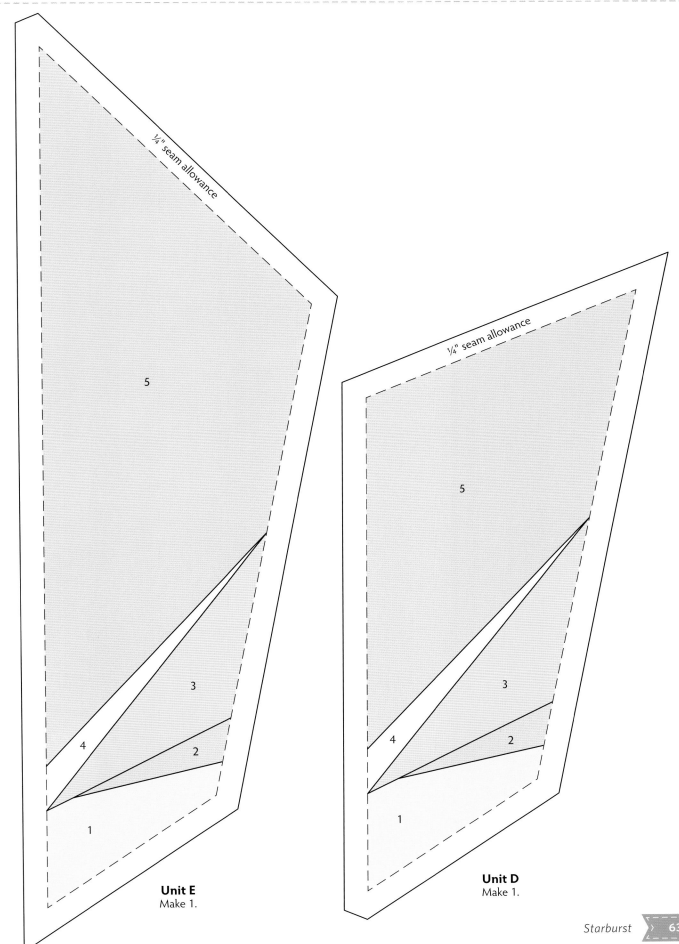

¼" seam allowance

5

3

4

2

1

Unit E
Make 1.

¼" seam allowance

5

3

4

2

1

Unit D
Make 1.

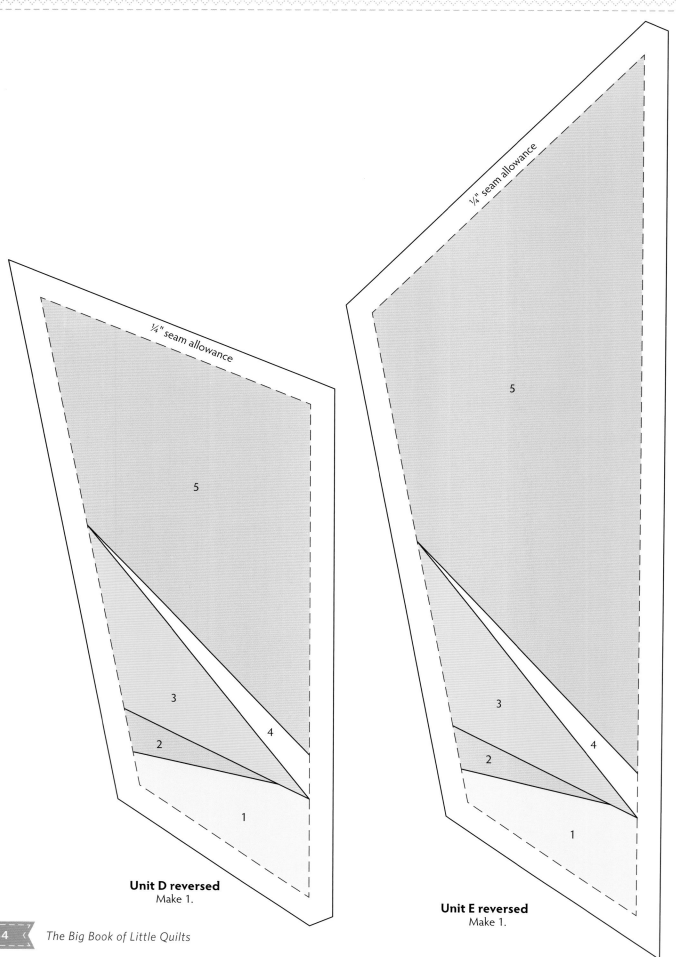

¼" seam allowance

5

3

4

2

1

Unit D reversed
Make 1.

¼" seam allowance

5

3

4

2

1

Unit E reversed
Make 1.

Mini Charm Star

What's not to love about 2½" squares—they're so adorable! Whether you use precuts or your personal supply of scraps, this little star quilt is a winner. It looks great in holiday prints too!

Finished quilt:
28½" × 28½"

Designed and made by Pat Sloan

Materials

Yardage is based on 42"-wide fabric.

60 squares, 2½" × 2½", of assorted red, cream, and tan prints for block*

12 squares, 2⅞" × 2⅞", of assorted red prints for block

¾ yard of tan print for block background and border

⅓ yard of red print for binding

1 yard of fabric for backing

32" × 32" piece of batting

*If you'd like to use precuts, note that a mini charm pack contains 40 squares, 2½" × 2½". If you use 2 mini charm packs, you'll have 20 squares left over for another project. Or, you can use 1 mini charm pack and cut an additional 20 squares from your stash.

Cutting

All measurements include ¼"-wide seam allowances.

From the tan print for background, cut:

4 squares, 6⅞" × 6⅞"; cut in half diagonally to yield 8 triangles

4 squares, 6½" × 6½"

2 strips, 2½" × 28½"

2 strips, 2½" × 24½"

From the red print for binding, cut:

4 strips, 2¼" × 42"

Assembling the Quilt Top

Mix up the 2½" squares to make four stacks of nine squares each, and set aside the remaining 24 squares for step 3. Press all seam allowances as indicated by the arrows.

1 Lay out the squares from one stack in a nine-patch arrangement as shown, arranging the squares as desired. Join the squares into rows. Join the rows to make a nine-patch unit. Make four units that each measure 6½" square.

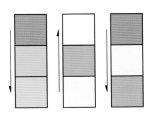

Make 4.

2 Cut the red 2⅞" squares in half diagonally to yield 24 triangles.

quadrant. Make four quadrants that each measure 12½" square.

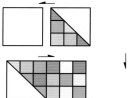

6 Lay out the quadrants as shown in the quilt assembly diagram below, rotating the quadrants to create the star design. Join the quadrants into rows, and then join the rows to make a Star block that measures 24½" square, including seam allowances.

7 Sew the tan 24½"-long strips to the top and bottom of the Star block. Sew the tan 28½"-long strips to the sides to complete the border.

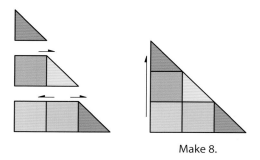

3 Lay out three 2½" squares and three triangles from step 2 as shown. Join the triangles and squares into rows. Join the rows. Make eight units.

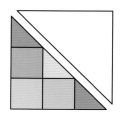

Make 8.

4 Sew a tan triangle to each unit from step 3 to make a star-point unit. Make eight star-point units that each measure 6½" square.

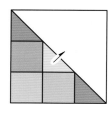

Make 8.

5 Lay out one nine-patch unit, two star-point units, and one tan 6½" square as shown. Join the pieces into rows, and then join the rows to make a

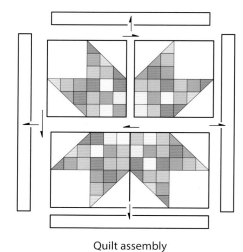

Quilt assembly

Finishing the Quilt

For help with the following finishing steps, go to ShopMartingale.com/HowtoQuilt for free, illustrated instructions.

1 Layer and baste the quilt top, batting, and backing. Quilt by hand or machine. The quilt shown uses straight-line quilting to frame the star.

2 Using the red 2¼"-wide strips, prepare and attach double-fold binding.

3 Add a hanging sleeve, if desired.

Teatime

Dress up a table or wall with a cheerful checkered quilt in a classic combination of red, cream, and blue. Use a pack of precut 5" squares that includes a variety of red-on-cream prints, or pull from your stash for an even scrappier touch.

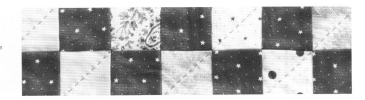

Finished quilt: 21¾" × 26¾"
Finished blocks: 3¾" × 3¾" and 3¾" × 5"

Designed and made by Laurie Simpson

Materials

Yardage is based on 42"-wide fabric. Charm squares are 5" × 5".

32 charm squares of assorted cream prints for blocks
3 charm squares of assorted red prints for accent
  squares
⅔ yard of red print for blocks and binding
¼ yard of blue plaid linen/cotton for rectangles*
⅔ yard of fabric for backing
26" × 31" piece of batting

*Depending on your fabric, more yardage might be needed for fussy cutting the rectangles so that you can center the plaid motif.

Cutting

All measurements include ¼"-wide seam allowances.

From *each* cream print charm square, cut:
2 strips, 1¾" × 5" (64 total)

From *each* red print charm square, cut:
1 square, 4¼" × 4¼" (3 total)

From the red print for blocks and binding, cut:
3 strips, 5" × 42"; crosscut into 65 strips, 1¾" × 5"
3 strips, 2" × 42"*

From the blue plaid, cut:
6 rectangles, 4¼" × 5½"**

*Feel free to cut wider binding strips if desired.
**Laurie fussy cut the blue plaid, centering the intersecting blue lines in each rectangle.

Making the Blocks

Press all seam allowances as indicated by the arrows.

1 Sew one cream strip between two red strips to make strip set A. Make 22. From each strip set, crosscut two 1¾"-wide segments for a total of 44 A segments.

Strip set A.
Make 22. Cut 44 segments, 1¾" × 4¼".

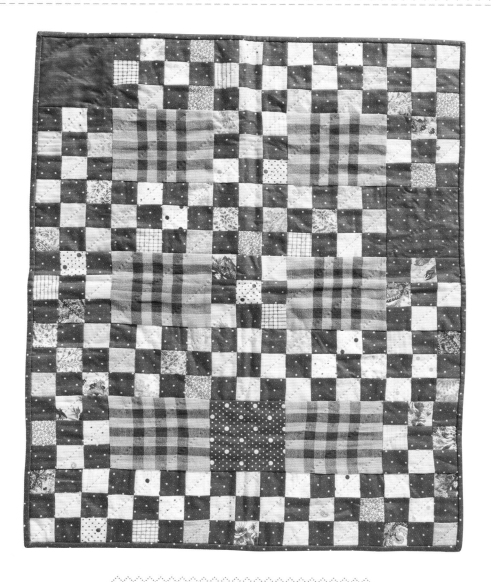

2 Sew one red strip between two cream strips to make strip set B. Make 21. From each strip set, crosscut two 1¾"-wide segments for a total of 42 B segments.

1¾"

Strip set B.
Make 21. Cut 42 segments, 1¾" × 4¼".

3 To make block A, arrange two A segments and one B segment in three rows as shown. Join the rows. Make 10 A blocks measuring 4¼" square.

Make 10 A blocks,
4¼" × 4¼".

4 To make block B, arrange two B segments and one A segment in three rows as shown. Join the rows. Make eight B blocks measuring 4¼" square.

Make 8 B blocks,
4¼" × 4¼".

5 To make block C, arrange two A segments and two B segments in four rows as shown. Join the rows. Make eight C blocks measuring 4¼" × 5½".

Make 8 C blocks,
4¼" × 5½".

Assembling the Quilt Top

1 Lay out the A, B, and C blocks along with the red squares and plaid rectangles in seven rows as shown in the quilt assembly diagram below.

2 Sew the pieces together into rows, and then join the rows.

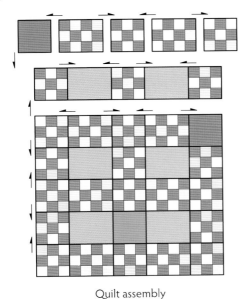

Quilt assembly

Finishing the Quilt

For help with the following finishing steps, go to ShopMartingale.com/HowtoQuilt for free, illustrated instructions.

1 Layer and baste the quilt top, batting, and backing. Quilt by hand or machine. The quilt shown is hand quilted in diagonal parallel lines placed 1¾" apart.

2 Using the red 2"-wide strips, prepare and attach double-fold binding.

3 Add a hanging sleeve, if desired.

Bayside

Scrappy triangles crisscrossing a field of green belie a simple secret: the quilt is composed of just six straight-set blocks. The open areas in the quilt center and borders provide a beautiful backdrop for feather quilting motifs, softening all those diagonal angles.

Finished quilt: 24½" × 33½"
Finished block: 9" × 9"

Designed and pieced by Betsy Chutchian; quilted by Sheri Mecom

Materials

Yardage is based on 42"-wide fabric.

60 squares, 2½" × 2½", of assorted light prints for blocks*

60 squares, 2½" × 2½", of assorted dark prints for blocks*

¾ yard of green print for blocks and outer border

½ yard of pink print for inner border and binding

⅞ yard of fabric for backing

29" × 38" piece of batting

Medium values can be used as lights or darks, depending on the fabrics they're paired with.

Cutting

All measurements include ¼"-wide seam allowances.

From the green print, cut:

3 strips, 3⅞" × 42"; crosscut into 24 squares, 3⅞" × 3⅞". Cut in half diagonally to yield 48 triangles.

2 strips, 2½" × 29½"

2 strips, 2½" × 24½"

From the pink print, cut:

4 strips, 2¼" × 42"

2 strips, 1½" × 27½"

2 strips, 1½" × 20½"

Making the Blocks

Press all seam allowances as indicated by the arrows.

1 Layer a light square on top of a dark square, right sides together. Draw a diagonal line from corner to corner on the light square. Sew ¼" from both sides of the drawn line. Cut on the line to yield two half-square-triangle units. Trim the units to measure 2" square. Make 72 half-square-triangle units.

Make 72 units,
2" × 2".

2 Layer two of the remaining print squares and trim them to 2⅜" square. Cut the layered squares in half diagonally to make two half-square triangles. Cut to make a total of 48 light and 48 dark triangles.

3 Lay out three half-square-triangle units, two dark triangles, and two light triangles as shown. Sew the pieces together into rows. Join the rows to make a center unit. Make 24 units. Sew a green triangle to each side of the center unit to make 24 block quadrants that measure 5" square, including seam allowances.

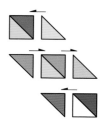

Make 24.

Make 24 units, 5" × 5".

4 Arrange four quadrants as shown. Sew them together into rows, and then join the rows to make a block. Make six blocks that measure 9½" square, including seam allowances.

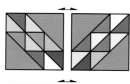

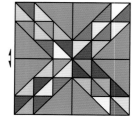

Make 6 blocks, 9½" × 9½".

Assembling the Quilt Top

1 Arrange the blocks in two vertical rows of three blocks each as shown in the quilt assembly diagram below.

2 Sew the blocks together into rows, and then join the rows. The quilt center should measure 18½" × 27½", including seam allowances.

3 Sew the pink 1½" × 27½" strips to opposite sides of the quilt center. Sew the pink 1½" × 20½" strips to the top and bottom. The quilt top should measure 20½" × 29½", including seam allowances.

4 Sew the green 2½" × 29½" strips to opposite sides of the quilt center. Sew the green 2½" × 24½" strips to the top and bottom. The quilt top should measure 24½" × 33½".

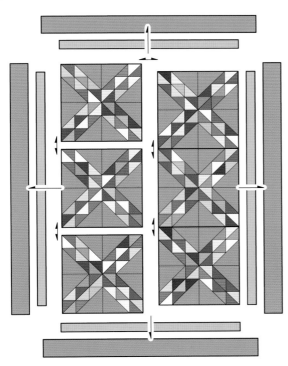

Quilt assembly

Finishing the Quilt

For help with the following finishing steps, go to ShopMartingale.com/HowtoQuilt for free, illustrated instructions.

1 Layer and baste the quilt top, batting, and backing. Quilt by hand or machine. The quilt shown is machine quilted with feather motifs.

2 Using the pink 2¼"-wide strips, prepare and attach double-fold binding.

3 Add a hanging sleeve, if desired.

Dainty Dishes

An 1880s Broken Dishes quilt inspired this reproduction. With the cheddar and gold prints in the sashing and the mismatched way these Dainty Dish blocks are constructed, it's easy to imagine the blocks were leftovers stitched together for a little girl's doll.

Finished quilt: 18" × 25½"
Finished blocks: 5" × 5" and 2½" × 2½"
Designed and made by Sheryl Johnson

Materials

Yardage is based on 42"-wide fabric.

⅔ yard *total* of assorted red, blue, pink, brown, tan, and cream prints for blocks
⅛ yard of cheddar solid for sashing
⅛ yard of cheddar print for sashing
⅛ yard of gold print for sashing
¼ yard of pink stripe for single-fold binding
⅝ yard of fabric for backing
22" × 30" piece of cream flannel or batting

Cutting

All measurements include ¼"-wide seam allowances.

From the assorted prints, cut:*
72 pairs of squares, 2¼" × 2¼" (144 total)

From the cheddar solid, cut:
6 rectangles, 3" × 5½"

From the cheddar print, cut:
5 rectangles, 3" × 5½"

From the gold print, cut:
6 rectangles, 3" × 5½"

From the pink stripe, cut:
3 strips, 1½" × 42"

*Cut extra 2¼" squares to mix and match for scrappy half-square-triangle units, if desired.

Making the Blocks

Press all seam allowances as indicated by the arrows.

1 Select two pairs of contrasting print 2¼" squares. Draw a diagonal line from corner to corner on the wrong side of the two lighter squares. Layer a marked square on an unmarked square, right sides together. Sew ¼" from both sides of the drawn line. Cut on the line to yield two half-square-triangle units. Trim to 1¾" square, including seam allowances. Make 144 units.

Make 144 units,
1¾" × 1¾".

2 Sew half-square-triangle units into two rows of two, and then join the rows to make 36 Dainty Dish units that measure 3" square, including seam allowances. You can use four matching units as shown, or two units each of different fabric pairings. The featured quilt uses a combination of both approaches.

Make 36 units,
3" × 3".

2 Sew together two gold print rectangles, one cheddar rectangle, and two 5½" blocks in alternating positions as shown to make row B. Repeat to make three B rows that measure 5½" × 18", including seam allowances.

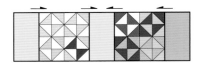

Row B.
Make 3 rows, 5½" × 18".

3 Lay out and then join the rows, matching the seam intersections. The completed quilt top should measure 18" × 25½".

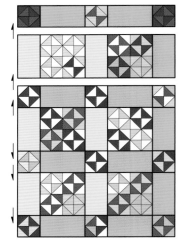

Quilt assembly

3 Sew together four Dainty Dish units to make a block that measures 5½" square, including seam allowances. Make six blocks.

Make 6 blocks,
5½" × 5½".

Assembling the Quilt Top

1 Sew together two cheddar rectangles and three single Dainty Dish units in alternating positions as shown to make row A. Repeat to make four A rows that measure 3" × 18", including seam allowances.

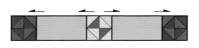

Row A.
Make 4 rows, 3" × 18".

Finishing the Quilt

For help with the following finishing steps, go to ShopMartingale.com/HowtoQuilt for free, illustrated instructions.

1 Layer and baste the quilt top, batting, and backing. Quilt by hand or machine. The quilt shown is hand quilted in a diagonal crosshatch pattern through the center of each block, continuing into the sashing.

2 Using the pink stripe 1½"-wide strips, prepare and attach single-fold binding (which some designers prefer to double-fold binding for small quilts).

3 Add a hanging sleeve, if desired.

Tilly's Basket Sampler

A bevy of baskets bring out the whimsical side of reproduction fabrics. Choose monochromatic dark prints of the same color for the setting triangles and outer border to frame and highlight the Basket blocks.

Finished quilt: 28½" × 37⅝"
Finished block: 5" × 5"

Designed and pieced by Carol Hopkins; quilted by Lisa Ramsey

Materials

Yardage is based on 42"-wide fabric. Specific requirements for each block are listed individually.

⅓ yard of pink print for sashing

17 assorted dark scraps, at least 6" × 6" each, for sashing stars

⅜ yard of dark brown check for setting triangles

¼ yard of burgundy print for inner border

¾ yard of brown print for outer border and binding

1¼ yards of fabric for backing

35" × 44" piece of batting

Cutting for Setting, Border, and Binding

All measurements include ¼"-wide seam allowances. Cutting instructions are listed individually for each Basket block.

From the pink print, cut:

4 strips, 2" × 42"; crosscut into 24 rectangles, 2" × 5½"

From *each* of the dark 6" × 6" scraps, cut:

1 square, 2" × 2" (17 total)
8 squares, 1¼" × 1¼" (136 total; 40 are extra)

From the dark brown check, cut:

2 squares, 11" × 11"; cut into quarters diagonally to yield 8 side triangles (2 are extra)
2 squares, 8" × 8"; cut in half diagonally to yield 4 corner triangles

From the burgundy print, cut:

4 strips, 1¼" × 42"

From the brown print, cut:

4 strips, 3½" × 42"
4 strips, 2" × 42"

Basket 1

For all blocks, press the seam allowances as indicated by the arrows or as otherwise specified. Make Basket 1 as follows.

MATERIALS

1 light scrap, at least 7" × 9"
1 brown scrap, at least 5" × 7"
1 gray scrap, at least 4" × 4"
1 red scrap, at least 4" × 6"

CUTTING

From the light scrap, cut:

1 square, 3⅜" × 3⅜"; cut in half diagonally to yield
    2 triangles (1 is extra)

2 rectangles, 1¾" × 3"

2 squares, 2⅛" × 2⅛"; cut in half diagonally to yield
    4 triangles

1 square, 1¾" × 1¾"

From the brown scrap, cut:

1 square, 3⅜" × 3⅜"; cut in half diagonally to yield
    2 triangles (1 is extra)

1 square, 2⅛" × 2⅛"; cut in half diagonally to yield
    2 triangles

From the gray scrap, cut:

1 square, 3⅜" × 3⅜"; cut in half diagonally to yield
    2 triangles (1 is extra)

From the red scrap, cut:

2 squares, 2⅛" × 2⅛"; cut in half diagonally to yield
    4 triangles

ASSEMBLING THE BLOCK

1 Sew a light 2⅛" triangle to a red 2⅛" triangle to make a half-square-triangle unit. Make four matching units measuring 1¾" square, including seam allowances.

Make 4 units,
1¾" × 1¾".

2 Sew the half-square-triangle units into pairs as shown. Make two units.

Make 1 of each unit,
1¾" × 3".

3 Sew a gray 3⅜" triangle to a brown 3⅜" triangle to make a half-square-triangle unit measuring 3" square, including seam allowances. Arrange the unit with the light 1¾" square and the units from step 2 as shown. Sew the pieces together into rows and then sew the rows together.

Make 1 unit,
4¼" × 4¼".

4 To make the side units, sew a brown 2⅛" triangle to a light 1¾" × 3" rectangle. Then make a mirror-image unit, sewing the triangle to the opposite end of a light rectangle.

Make 1 of each unit.

5 Sew the side units to the bottom and right edges of the basket unit as shown on page 82. Sew a light 3⅜" triangle to the bottom of the basket to

complete a block measuring 5½" square, including seam allowances.

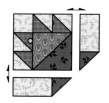

Basket 1.
Make 1, 5½" × 5½".

Basket 2

Make Basket 2 as follows.

MATERIALS

1 light scrap, at least 7" × 9"
1 black scrap, at least 5" × 7"
1 green scrap, at least 5" × 6"

CUTTING

From the light scrap, cut:
1 square, 3⅜" × 3⅜"; cut in half diagonally to yield
   2 triangles
2 rectangles, 1¾" × 3"
2 squares, 2⅛" × 2⅛"; cut in half diagonally to yield
   4 triangles

From the black scrap, cut:
1 square, 3⅜" × 3⅜"; cut in half diagonally to yield
   2 triangles (1 is extra)
1 square, 2⅛" × 2⅛"; cut in half diagonally to yield
   2 triangles

From the green scrap, cut:
2 squares, 2⅛" × 2⅛"; cut in half diagonally to yield
   4 triangles
1 square, 1¾" × 1¾"

ASSEMBLING THE BLOCK

1 Sew a light 2⅛" triangle to a green 2⅛" triangle to make a half-square-triangle unit. Make four matching units measuring 1¾" square, including seam allowances. Sew the units into pairs as shown.

Make 1 of each unit,
1¾" × 3".

2 Sew a light 3⅜" triangle to a black 3⅜" triangle to make a half-square-triangle unit measuring 3" square, including seam allowances. Arrange the unit with the green 1¾" square and the units from step 1 as shown. Sew the pieces together into rows and then sew the rows together to make a basket unit measuring 4¼" square, including seam allowances.

Make 1 unit,
4¼" × 4¼".

3 To make the side units, sew a black 2⅛" triangle to a light 1¾" × 3" rectangle. Repeat to make a mirror-image unit.

Make 1 of each unit.

4 Arrange the basket unit, the side units, and a light 3⅜" triangle as shown. Join the pieces to complete a block measuring 5½" square, including seam allowances.

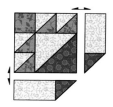

Basket 2.
Make 1, 5½" × 5½".

Basket 3

Make Basket 3 as follows.

MATERIALS

1 light scrap, at least 8" × 10"
1 green scrap, at least 5" × 7"
23 assorted medium or dark scraps (collectively referred to as "dark"), at least 1" × 1" each

CUTTING

From the light scrap, cut:

1 square, 2⅞" × 2⅞"; cut in half diagonally to yield 2
   triangles (1 is extra)
2 rectangles, 1½" × 3½"
3 squares, 1⅜" × 1⅜"; cut in half diagonally to yield 6
   triangles
20 squares, 1" × 1"

From the green scrap, cut:

1 square, 3⅞" × 3⅞"; cut in half diagonally to yield 2
   triangles (1 is extra)
1 square, 1⅞" × 1⅞"; cut in half diagonally to yield 2
   triangles

From *each* of the dark scraps, cut:

1 square, 1" × 1" (23 total)

ASSEMBLING THE BLOCK

1 Arrange the 23 dark 1" squares, 20 light 1"
squares, and six light 1⅜" triangles as shown.
Sew the pieces together into rows and press. Sew the
rows together, pressing after adding each row.

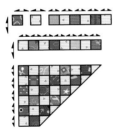

2 Sew a green 3⅞" triangle to the step 1 unit to
make a basket unit measuring 4½" square,
including seam allowances.

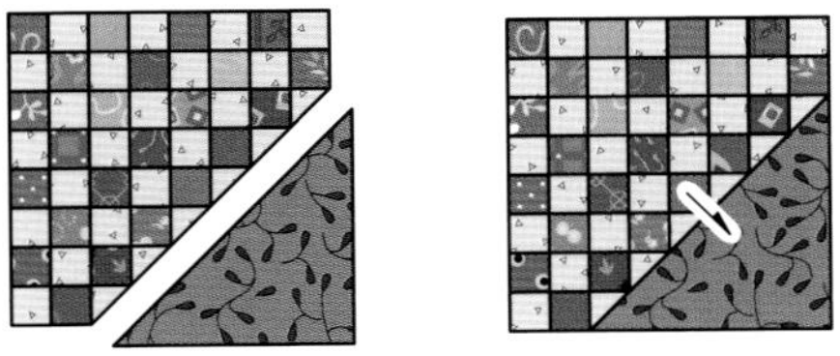

Make 1 unit,
4½" × 4½".

3 To make the side units, sew a green 1⅞" triangle
to a light 1½" × 3½" rectangle. Repeat to make a
mirror-image unit.

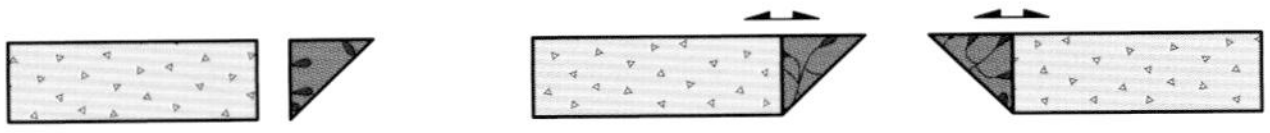

Make 1 of each unit.

4 Sew the side units to the bottom and right edges
of the basket unit as shown. Sew a light 2⅞"
triangle to the bottom of the basket to complete a block
measuring 5½" square, including seam allowances.

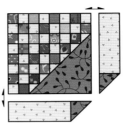 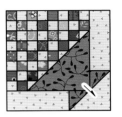

Basket 3.
Make 1, 5½" × 5½".

Basket 4

Make Basket 4 as follows.

MATERIALS

1 light scrap, at least 6" × 7"
1 brown scrap, at least 5" × 7"
1 gray scrap, at least 4" × 6"

CUTTING

From the light scrap, cut:

1 square, 3⅜" × 3⅜"; cut in half diagonally to yield
   2 triangles
2 rectangles, 1¾" × 3"
1 square, 2⅛" × 2⅛"; cut in half diagonally to yield
   2 triangles (1 is extra)

From the brown scrap, cut:

1 square, 3⅜" × 3⅜"; cut in half diagonally to yield
   2 triangles (1 is extra)
1 square, 2⅛" × 2⅛"; cut in half diagonally to yield
   2 triangles

From the gray scrap, cut:

2 rectangles, 1¾" × 3"
1 square, 2⅛" × 2⅛"; cut in half diagonally to yield
   2 triangles (1 is extra)

ASSEMBLING THE BLOCK

1 Join light and gray 2⅛" triangles to make a
half-square-triangle unit measuring 1¾" square,
including seam allowances. Join light and brown 3⅜"
triangles to make a half-square-triangle unit measuring
3" square, including seam allowances.

2 Arrange the two gray 1¾" × 3" rectangles and the units from step 1 as shown. Sew the pieces together into rows and then sew the rows together to make a basket unit measuring 4¼" square, including seam allowances.

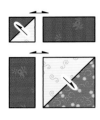

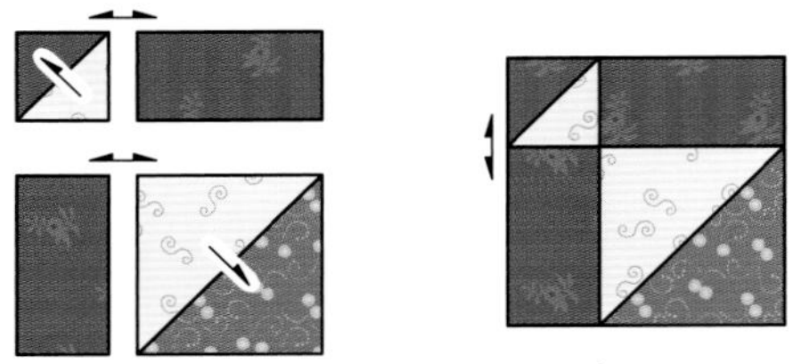

Make 1 unit,
4¼" × 4¼".

3 To make the side units, sew a brown 2⅛" triangle to a light 1¾" × 3" rectangle. Repeat to make a mirror-image unit.

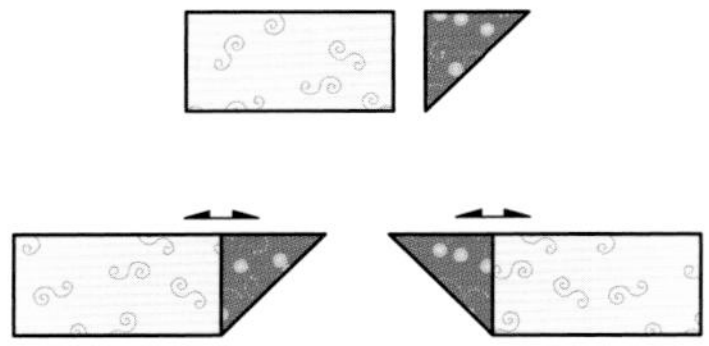

Make 1 of each unit.

4 Sew the side units to the bottom and right edges of the basket unit. Sew a light 3⅜" triangle to the bottom to complete a block measuring 5½" square, including seam allowances.

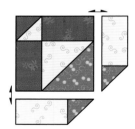 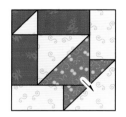

Basket 4.
Make 1, 5½" × 5½".

Basket 5

Make Basket 5 as follows.

MATERIALS

1 light scrap, at least 8" × 9"
1 brown scrap, at least 5" × 8"
1 pink scrap, at least 3" × 7"

CUTTING

From the light scrap, cut:
2 squares, 2⅞" × 2⅞"; cut in half diagonally to yield 4 triangles (1 is extra)
2 rectangles, 1½" × 3½"
3 squares, 1⅞" × 1⅞"; cut in half diagonally to yield 6 triangles
1 square, 1½" × 1½"

From the brown scrap, cut:
1 square, 2⅞" × 2⅞"; cut in half diagonally to yield 2 triangles (1 is extra)
4 squares, 1⅞" × 1⅞"; cut in half diagonally to yield 8 triangles

From the pink scrap, cut:
3 squares, 1⅞" × 1⅞"; cut in half diagonally to yield 6 triangles

ASSEMBLING THE BLOCK

1 Sew a light 1⅞" triangle to a pink 1⅞" triangle to make a half-square-triangle unit. Make four matching units measuring 1½" square, including seam allowances.

2 Sew together the light 1½" square, two units from step 1, and a light 1⅞" triangle as shown.

Make 1 unit.

3 Join two step 1 units and a light 1⅞" triangle as shown.

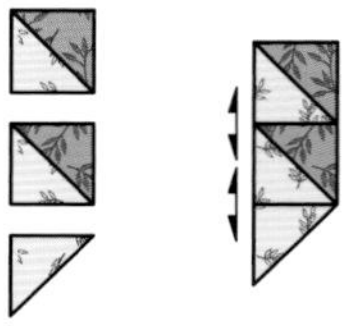

Make 1 unit.

4 Arrange the pieced units with a light 2⅞" triangle as shown. Sew the pieces together into rows and then sew the rows together.

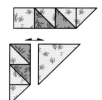 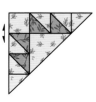

5 Sew a pink 1⅞" triangle to a brown 1⅞" triangle to make a half-square-triangle unit. Make two units measuring 1½" square, including seam allowances. Sew brown 1⅞" triangles to both pink edges of the half-square-triangle units. Trim off the dog-ear points.

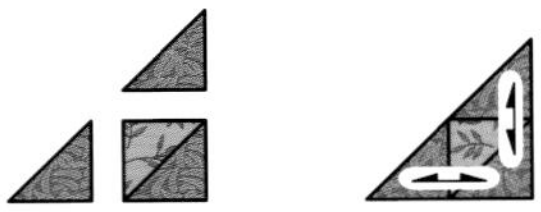

Make 2 units.

6 Sew a light 2⅞" triangle to a brown 2⅞" triangle to make a half-square-triangle unit measuring 2½" square, including seam allowances.

7 Sew the units from step 5 to the light edges of the unit from step 6.

Make 1 unit.

8 Join the units from steps 4 and 7.

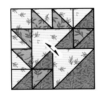

Make 1 unit,
4½" × 4½".

9 To make the side units, sew a brown 1⅞" triangle to a light 1½" × 3½" rectangle. Repeat to make a mirror-image unit.

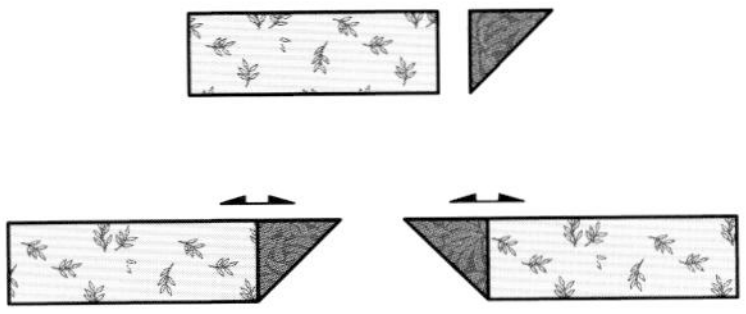

Make 1 of each.

10 Sew the side units to the bottom and right edges of the basket unit. Sew a light 2⅞" triangle to the bottom of the basket to make a block measuring 5½" square, including seam allowances.

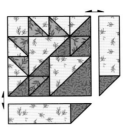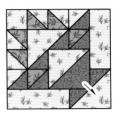

Basket 5.
Make 1, 5½" × 5½".

Basket 6

Make Basket 6 as follows.

MATERIALS

1 light scrap, at least 8" × 8"
1 black scrap, at least 5" × 7"
1 red scrap, at least 5" × 7"

CUTTING

From the light scrap, cut:
1 square, 2⅞" × 2⅞"; cut in half diagonally to yield
　　2 triangles (1 is extra)
2 rectangles, 1½" × 3½"
3 squares, 1⅞" × 1⅞"; cut in half diagonally to yield
　　6 triangles
1 square, 1½" × 1½"

From the black scrap, cut:
1 square, 3⅞" × 3⅞"; cut in half diagonally to yield
　　2 triangles (1 is extra)
2 squares, 1⅞" × 1⅞"; cut in half diagonally to yield
　　4 triangles

From the red scrap, cut:
1 square, 3⅞" × 3⅞"; cut in half diagonally to yield
　　2 triangles (1 is extra)
2 squares, 1⅞" × 1⅞"; cut in half diagonally to yield
　　4 triangles

Basket 1

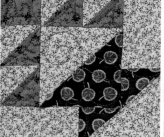
Basket 2

Basket 3

Basket 4

ASSEMBLING THE BLOCK

1 Sew a red 3⅞" triangle to a black 3⅞" triangle to make a half-square-triangle unit measuring 3½" square, including seam allowances.

2 Sew together light and red 1⅞" triangles to make four half-square-triangle units, and join light and black 1⅞" triangles to make two half-square-triangle units. Each unit should measure 1½" square, including seam allowances.

3 To make the side units, sew together the light 1½" square, two red half-square-triangle units, and one black half-square-triangle unit as shown. Make a second unit, but omit the light square.

Make 1 unit,
1½" × 4½".

Make 1 unit,
1½" × 3½".

4 Sew the units from step 3 to the top and left edges of the red/black half-square-triangle unit from step 1 to make a unit measuring 4½" square, including seam allowances.

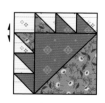

Make 1 unit,
4½" × 4½".

5 To make the side units, sew a black 1⅞" triangle to a light 1½" × 3½" rectangle. Repeat to make a mirror-image unit.

Make 1 of each.

6 Sew the side units to the bottom and right edges of the basket unit. Sew a light 2⅞" triangle to the bottom of the basket to complete a block measuring 5½" square, including seam allowances.

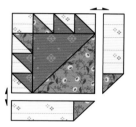 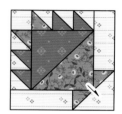

Basket 6.
Make 1, 5½" × 5½".

Basket 7

Make Basket 7 as follows.

MATERIALS

1 light scrap, at least 9" × 10"

1 black scrap, at least 5" × 7"

10 assorted medium or dark scraps (collectively referred to as "dark"), at least 3" × 3" each

CUTTING

From the light scrap, cut:

1 square, 2⅞" × 2⅞"; cut in half diagonally to yield 2 triangles (1 is extra)

2 rectangles, 1½" × 3½"

7 squares, 1⅞" × 1⅞"; cut in half diagonally to yield 14 triangles (1 is extra)

| *Basket 5* | *Basket 6* | *Basket 7* | *Basket 8* |

From the black scrap, cut:

1 square, 3⅞" × 3⅞"; cut in half diagonally to yield
    2 triangles (1 is extra)

1 square, 1⅞" × 1⅞"; cut in half diagonally to yield
    2 triangles

From *each* of the dark scraps, cut:

1 square, 1⅞" × 1⅞"; cut in half diagonally to yield
    2 triangles (20 total; 10 are extra)

ASSEMBLING THE BLOCK

1 Sew a dark 1⅞" triangle to a light 1⅞" triangle to make a half-square-triangle unit. Make 10 units measuring 1½" square, including seam allowances.

2 Arrange the units from step 1 with three light 1⅞" triangles as shown. Sew the units into rows and press. Sew the rows together, pressing after adding each row.

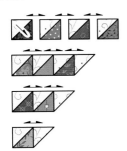
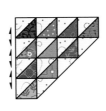

3 Sew a black 3⅞" triangle to the unit from step 2.

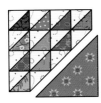

Make 1 unit,
4½" × 4½".

4 To make the side units, sew a black 1⅞" triangle to a light 1½" × 3½" rectangle. Repeat to make a mirror-image unit.

Make 1 of each.

5 Sew the side units to the bottom and right edges of the basket unit as shown. Sew a light 2⅞" triangle to the bottom of the basket to complete a block measuring 5½" square, including seam allowances.

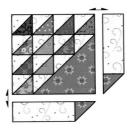
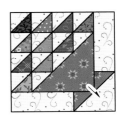

Basket 7.
Make 1, 5½" × 5½".

Basket 8

Make Basket 8 as follows.

MATERIALS

1 light scrap, at least 7" × 10"

1 blue scrap, at least 5" × 7"

1 brown scrap, at least 3" × 5"

1 cheddar scrap, at least 3" × 5"

CUTTING

From the light scrap, cut:

1 square, 3⅜" × 3⅜"; cut in half diagonally
    to yield 2 triangles (1 is extra)

4 rectangles, 1¾" × 3"

1 square, 1¾" × 1¾"

Continued on page 88

Continued from page 87

From the blue scrap, cut:

4 squares, 1¾" × 1¾"

1 square, 2⅛" × 2⅛"; cut in half diagonally
to yield 2 triangles

From the brown scrap, cut:

2 squares, 1¾" × 1¾"

From the cheddar scrap, cut:

2 squares, 1¾" × 1¾"

ASSEMBLING THE BLOCK

1 Make a flying-geese unit with two blue 1¾"
squares and one light 1¾" × 3" rectangle as
shown. Make two matching units.

Make 2 units,
1¾" × 3".

2 Sew two brown 1¾" squares and two cheddar
1¾" squares together to make a four-patch unit
measuring 3" square, including seam allowances.

Make 1 unit,
3" × 3".

3 Arrange the light 1¾" square with the flying-
geese and four-patch units. Sew the pieces into
rows and then sew the rows together to make a unit
measuring 4¼" square, including seam allowances.

Make 1 unit,
4¼" × 4¼".

4 To make the side units, sew a blue 2⅛" triangle
to a light 1¾" × 3" rectangle as shown. Repeat to
make a mirror-image unit.

Make 1 of each unit.

5 Sew the side units to the bottom and right edges
of the basket unit. Sew a light 3⅜" triangle to the
bottom to complete a block measuring 5½" square,
including seam allowances.

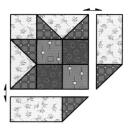 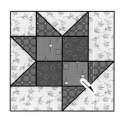

Basket 8.
Make 1, 5½" × 5½".

Assembling the Quilt Top

1 Arrange the blocks, sashing rectangles, sashing
squares, and setting triangles as shown.

2 Working with one sashing rectangle at a time, sew two 1¼" squares that match the adjacent sashing square to one end of a pink 2" × 5½" rectangle. Repeat on the other end of the same sashing rectangle using 1¼" squares that match the 2" sashing square they touch. Make 24 sashing rectangle units.

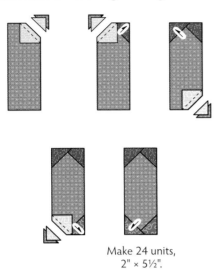

Make 24 units,
2" × 5½".

3 Sew the blocks, sashing rectangles, and sashing squares together into rows as shown.

4 Sew the block rows and sashing strips together and press after adding each row. Add the side setting triangles to the rows; press.

5 Center the brown check corner triangles and sew them to the quilt.

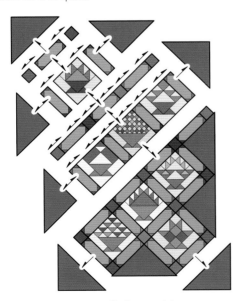

Quilt assembly

6 Trim and square up the quilt top, leaving ¼" seam allowances beyond the corners of the blocks.

7 For the inner border, measure the length of the quilt top through the center and trim two of the burgundy 1¼"-wide strips to this measurement. Sew the strips to the sides of the quilt top and press the seam allowances toward the border.

8 Measure the width of the quilt top through the center, including the just-added border pieces, and trim the two remaining burgundy 1¼"-wide strips to this measurement. Sew the strips to the top and bottom of the quilt and press the seam allowances toward the border.

9 For the outer border, repeat steps 7 and 8 using the brown 3½"-wide strips.

Finishing the Quilt Top

For help with the following finishing steps, go to ShopMartingale.com/HowtoQuilt for free, illustrated instructions.

1 Layer and baste the quilt top, batting, and backing. Quilt by hand or machine. The quilt shown is machine quilted with leaves and scrolls in the blocks, flowers in the side triangles, and feathers in the border.

2 Using the brown 2"-wide strips, prepare and attach double-fold binding.

3 Add a hanging sleeve, if desired.

Little Strippy

If you like working with tiny pieces, put on your magnifiers and prepare for some serious fun. These Nine Patch blocks finish at only 1½" square! They look so cute in their three vertical rows, they have no trouble holding their own against the dark, warm border prints.

Finished quilt: 12⅜" × 15⅛"
Finished block: 1½" × 1½"

Designed by Kathleen Tracy;
pieced and hand quilted by Marian Edwards

Materials

Yardage is based on 42"-wide fabric. Fat quarters are 18" × 21".

⅛ yard *total* of assorted light prints for blocks
⅛ yard *total* of assorted medium and dark prints for blocks
⅛ yard of light blue print for setting triangles
¼ yard of green print for sashing strips and single-fold binding
⅛ yard of dark blue print for border
⅛ yard of rust print for border
1 square, 6" × 6", of brown print for border corners
1 fat quarter of fabric for backing
16" × 19" piece of low-loft cotton batting

Cutting

All measurements include ¼"-wide seam allowances.

From the assorted light prints, cut:
15 sets of 4 matching squares, 1" × 1" (60 total)

From the assorted medium and dark prints, cut:
15 sets of 4 matching squares, 1" × 1" (60 total)
15 contrasting squares, 1" × 1"

From the light blue print, cut:
6 squares, 3½" × 3½"; cut into quarters diagonally to yield 24 setting triangles
6 squares, 2" × 2"; cut in half diagonally to yield 12 corner triangles

From the green print, cut:
2 strips, 1¼" × 42"
2 strips, 1¼" × 11⅛"

From the dark blue print, cut:
2 strips, 2½" × 11⅛"

From the rust print, cut:
2 strips, 2½" × 8⅜"

From the brown print, cut:
4 squares, 2½" × 2½"

Assembling the Quilt Top

1 Lay out five blocks, eight large light blue triangles, and four small light blue corner triangles as shown. Sew together in a vertical row. Trim and square up the row, leaving ¼" beyond the points of all the blocks for seam allowances. Make three rows that measure approximately 2⅝" × 11⅛".

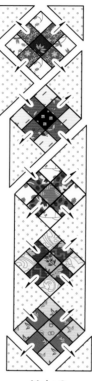

Make 3.

2 Sew the block rows from step 1 and the green 1¼" × 11⅛" strips together as shown in the quilt assembly diagram on page 93 to make the quilt center that measures 8⅜" × 11⅛".

Making the Blocks

Press all seam allowances as indicated by the arrows.

Choose four matching light squares, four matching medium or dark squares, and one contrasting square. Lay out the squares in three rows as shown. Sew the squares together into rows. Join the rows. The blocks should measure 2" square, including seam allowances. Make 15 blocks.

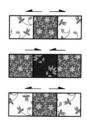

Make 15.

The Big Book of Little Quilts

3 Sew the dark blue strips to opposite sides of the quilt. Sew a brown square to each end of a rust strip. Make two and sew them to the top and bottom of the quilt.

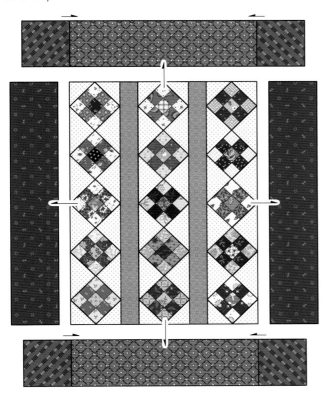

Quilt assembly

Finishing the Quilt

For help with the following finishing steps, go to ShopMartingale.com/HowtoQuilt for free, illustrated instructions.

1 Layer and baste the quilt top, batting, and backing. Quilt by hand or machine. The quilt shown is quilted with an X through the blocks, double parallel lines in the sashing strips, and double parallel lines in the borders with a zigzag line between them. Outline quilting is used for the setting triangles and a double X is added in the corner blocks.

2 Using the green 1¼" × 42" strips, prepare and attach single-fold binding (which some designers prefer to double-fold binding for small quilts).

3 Add a hanging sleeve, if desired.

Dixie

This complex-looking quilt is made with just three simple components—four patches, hourglass units, and triangle squares. Whether you choose Civil War reproduction fabrics or lots of scraps, you'll have fun putting this project together bit by bit.

Finished quilt: 40½" × 40½"
Finished blocks: 4" × 4"

Designed and made by Mary Etherington and Connie Tesene

Materials

Yardage is based on 42"-wide fabric.

⅛ yard *each* of 24 assorted dark prints in navy, blue, light blue, teal, brown, red, maroon, red-orange, and black for blocks and pieced border

⅛ yard *each* of 24 assorted light prints in white, cream, tan, gold, medium red, blue, and brown for blocks and pieced border

⅜ yard of tan print for binding

2⅝ yards of fabric for backing

44" × 44" piece of batting

Cutting

All measurements include ¼"-wide seam allowances.

From the dark prints, cut:

82 squares, 3¼" × 3¼"; cut into quarters diagonally to yield 328 triangles

40 sets of 2 matching squares, 2½" × 2½" (80 total)

38 squares, 2⅞" × 2⅞"; cut in half diagonally to yield 76 triangles

From the light prints, cut:

82 squares, 3¼" × 3¼"; cut into quarters diagonally to yield 328 triangles

40 sets of 2 matching squares, 2½" × 2½" (80 total)

38 squares, 2⅞" × 2⅞"; cut in half diagonally to yield 76 triangles

From the tan print, cut:

5 strips, 2¼" × 42"

Making the Hourglass Blocks

Use one light and one dark print for each unit. Press all seam allowances as indicated by the arrows or as otherwise specified.

1 Join two light triangles and two dark triangles to make an hourglass unit. The unit should measure 2½" square, including seam allowances. Make 164 units.

Make 164.

Making the Four Patch Blocks

Sew two matching light 2½" squares and two matching dark 2½" squares together to make a Four Patch block as shown. Make 40 blocks.

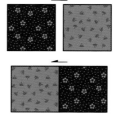 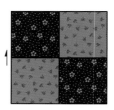

Make 40.

Assembling the Quilt Top

1 Sew a pair of light and dark 2⅞" triangles together. Make 76 half-square-triangle units.

Make 76.

2 Sew 18 half-square-triangle units together, orienting the dark triangles in the same direction to make the top border. Sew 18 units together, reversing the direction of the dark triangles, to make the bottom border. Sew 20 half-square-triangle units together in the same manner to make a side border. Make two side borders.

Top border

Bottom border

Side borders
Make 2.

Mix It Up

You can use the same prints in an hourglass unit or, for a more antique look, mix up some of the fabrics as in the quilt shown. You can also sew a few Hourglass blocks together incorrectly.

2 Randomly select four hourglass units and lay them out in a four-patch arrangement, rotating the units so that the light and dark triangles alternate positions. Sew the units together into rows. Sew the rows together and press the seam allowances in one direction. Make 41 blocks.

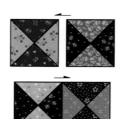 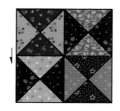

Make 41.

3 Alternating Hourglass and Four Patch blocks, arrange the blocks in nine rows of nine blocks each. Rearrange the blocks until you are pleased with the color placement.

4 Sew the blocks together into rows, pressing the seam allowances toward the Four Patch blocks. Join the rows and press the seam allowances in one direction.

5 Sew the top, bottom, and side border strips to the quilt top, orienting the strips as shown in the quilt-assembly diagram.

Finishing the Quilt

For help with the following finishing steps, go to ShopMartingale.com/HowtoQuilt for free, illustrated instructions.

1 Layer and baste the quilt top, batting, and backing. Quilt by hand or machine.

2 Using the tan 2¼"-wide strips, prepare and attach double-fold binding.

3 Add a hanging sleeve, if desired.

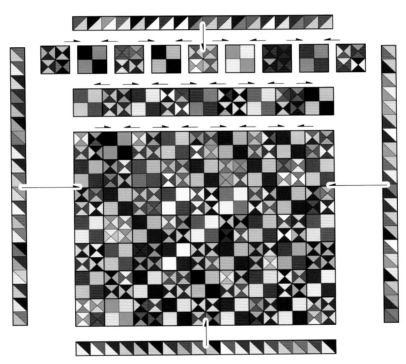

Quilt assembly

Tic-Tac-Toe

Quiltmaker Jo loved these blocks of cute 3" nine-patch units, but when she paired them with the setting fabric, she felt they needed a little extra "something." The addition of narrow sashing puts the nine-patches in the spotlight where they belong.

Finished quilt: 36½" × 36½"
Finished block: 6½" × 6½"

Designed and made by Jo Morton

Materials

Yardage is based on 42"-wide fabric.

⅓ yard *total* of assorted brown A prints for blocks

⅝ yard *total* of assorted pink prints for blocks and Sawtooth border

⅝ yard of light print for blocks and Sawtooth border

¼ yard of blue print for blocks and cornerstones

¼ yard of gold print for blocks

¾ yard of brown B print for setting squares, triangles, and single-fold binding

1 yard of pink floral for outer border

1¼ yards of fabric for backing

41" × 41" piece of batting

Cutting

All measurements include ¼"-wide seam allowances. Each block contains light, blue, and gold fabrics, along with a variety of either brown or pink fabrics. Repeat the cutting instructions to make 5 brown blocks and 4 pink blocks (9 blocks total).

FOR 1 BLOCK

From the assorted brown A or pink prints, cut:
16 squares, 1½" × 1½"

From the light print, cut:
16 squares, 1½" × 1½"

From the blue print, cut:
4 squares, 1½" × 1½"
1 square, 1" × 1"

From the gold print, cut:
4 rectangles, 1" × 3½"

FOR THE SAWTOOTH BORDER

From the light print, cut:
12 squares, 4½" × 4½"

From the assorted pink prints, cut:
12 squares, 4½" × 4½"

FOR THE SETTING SQUARES AND TRIANGLES

From the brown B print, cut:
2 squares, 11" × 11"; cut into quarters diagonally to yield 8 side triangles
2 squares, 6" × 6"; cut in half diagonally to yield 4 corner triangles
4 squares, 7" × 7"

Continued on page 100

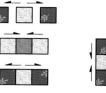

toward the brown and blue squares; press the clipped intersections open. Make a total of 20 nine-patch units.

Make 20 units,
3½" × 3½".

2 Repeat step 1 using four pink squares, four light squares, and one blue 1½" square to make 16 nine-patch units.

Make 16 units,
3½" × 3½".

3 Lay out four brown A nine-patch units, four gold 1" × 3½" rectangles, and one blue 1" square in three rows as shown. Sew the pieces together into rows. Join the rows to make a block measuring 7" square. Make a total of five blocks.

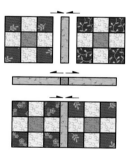
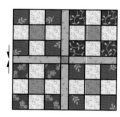

Make 5 blocks,
7" × 7".

4 Lay out four pink nine-patch units, four gold 1" × 3½" rectangles, and one blue 1" square in three rows as shown. Sew the pieces together into rows. Join the rows to make a block measuring 7" square. Make a total of four blocks.

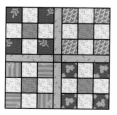

Make 4 blocks,
7" × 7".

Continued from page 99

FOR THE OUTER BORDER, CORNERSTONES, AND BINDING

From the *lengthwise* grain of the pink floral, cut:*
4 strips, 3½" × 30½"

From the blue print, cut:
4 squares, 3½" × 3½"

From the brown B print, cut:
4 strips, 1⅛" × 42"

*Jo recommends cutting these pieces on the lengthwise grain of the fabric (parallel to the selvage) because it has the least amount of stretch and will give you nice, straight edges.

Making the Blocks

Press all seam allowances as indicated by the arrows.

1 Lay out four brown A squares, four light squares, and one blue 1½" square in three rows as shown above right. Sew the squares together into rows. Join the rows to complete a nine-patch unit measuring 3½" square. At the seam intersections, cut through both layers of the seam allowance, right up to but not through the stitching. Press the seam allowances

Making the Sawtooth Border

1 Draw a diagonal line from corner to corner in both directions on the wrong side of each light 4½" square.

2 Lay a marked light square on top of a pink 4½" square, right sides together. Sew a scant ¼" from each side of the drawn lines.

3 Cut the sewn squares apart *first* horizontally and then vertically to make four segments.

4 Cut each segment apart on the drawn diagonal line to make eight half-square-triangle units (each segment yields two half-square-triangle units). Trim each unit to measure 1¾" square. Make a total of 96 units. (You'll use 92.)

Make 96
(4 are extra).

5 Sew 22 half-square-triangle units together as shown to make a 28"-long side border strip. Press the seam allowances open to reduce bulk. Repeat to make a second side border strip.

Make 2 side borders.

6 Sew 24 half-square-triangle units together as shown to make a 30½"-long top border strip. Press the seam allowances open. Repeat to make a bottom border strip.

Make 2 top/bottom borders.

Assembling the Quilt Top

1 Lay out the blocks and brown B setting squares with the brown B side and corner triangles in diagonal rows as shown.

2 Sew the pieces together into rows. Join the rows, matching the seam intersections. Add the corner triangles last. At the seam intersections, cut through both layers of the seam allowance, right up to but not through the stitching. Press the seam allowances toward the brown B squares and triangles; press the clipped intersections open. Trim and square up the quilt top to measure 28" square, including seam allowances, making sure to leave a ¼" seam allowance beyond all points.

Quilt assembly

3 Sew the 28"-long Sawtooth border strips to opposite sides of the quilt top with the pink prints adjoining the quilt center as shown in the diagram below. Sew the 30½"-long Sawtooth border strips to the top and bottom of the quilt top. The quilt top should measure 30½" square, including seam allowances.

4 Sew pink floral 30½"-long strips to opposite sides of the quilt top. Sew a blue 3½" square to each end of the remaining pink floral strips. Sew these strips to the top and bottom of the quilt top.

Finishing the Quilt

For help with the following finishing steps, go to ShopMartingale.com/HowtoQuilt for free, illustrated instructions.

1 Layer and baste the quilt top, batting, and backing. Quilt by hand or machine. The quilt shown is machine quilted in the ditch. A squared double-feather wreath is quilted in the setting squares and a half-square feather wreath is quilted in the side triangles. The two borders are treated as one and quilted in a crosshatch design, with the spacing determined by the Sawtooth border.

2 Using the 1⅛"-wide brown B strips, prepare and attach single-fold binding (which some designers prefer to double-fold binding for small quilts).

3 Add a hanging sleeve, if desired.

Making the Borders Fit

If the Sawtooth border strips aren't a perfect fit, you'll need to adjust the seam allowances in a few places. To make a strip slightly longer, use a narrower seam allowance. If a border is a little too long, use a wider seam allowance. Be sure to spread the adjustments across the entire border strip and it will work out just fine.

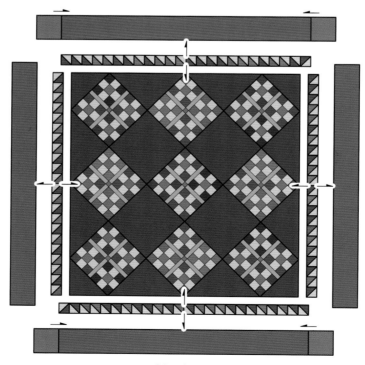

Adding borders

Windowpane

Inspired by some simple blocks in an antique quilt, this little creation includes one block with mismatched squares for a quirky touch. Pleasing blue prints and a few bright pink squares perk things up and provide a nice vintage look.

Finished quilt: 17" × 17"
Finished block: 3½" × 3½"

Designed and made by Kathleen Tracy

Materials

Yardage is based on 42"-wide fabric.

⅓ yard *total* of assorted light, medium, and dark prints for blocks
⅛ yard of brown print for inner border
¼ yard of blue print for outer border
⅛ yard of red print for single-fold binding
⅝ yard of fabric for backing
20" × 20" piece of low-loft cotton batting

Cutting

All measurements include ¼"-wide seam allowances.

From the assorted light, medium, and dark prints, cut:
32 squares, 2" × 2" (8 sets of 4 matching squares)
4 squares, 2" × 2" (2 sets of 2 matching squares)
36 rectangles, 1" × 2" (9 sets of 4 matching rectangles)
9 squares, 1" × 1" (assorted)

From the brown print, cut:
2 strips, 1½" × 13"
2 strips, 1½" × 11"

From the blue print, cut:
2 strips, 2½" × 17"
2 strips, 2½" × 13"

From the red print, cut:
2 strips, 1¼" × 42"

Making the Blocks

Press all seam allowances as indicated by the arrows.

For each block, choose four matching 2" squares from one light, medium, or dark print and four matching 1" × 2" rectangles from a different print. The rectangles should contrast with the squares. Choose a 1" square from a third fabric. Lay out the squares and rectangles in three rows as shown. Sew the pieces together into rows. Join the rows. Make eight blocks that measure 4" square. For the ninth block, use two different pairs of 2" squares.

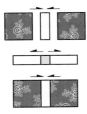

Make 9.

3 Sew the brown 1½" × 11" strips to opposite sides of the quilt top. Sew the brown 1½" × 13" strips to the top and bottom.

4 Sew the blue 2½" × 13" strips to opposite sides of the quilt top. Sew the blue 2½" × 17" strips to the top and bottom of the quilt.

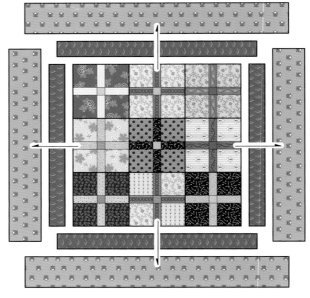

Quilt assembly

Assembling the Quilt Top

1 Lay out the blocks in three rows of three blocks each, rearranging the blocks until you find a pleasing arrangement.

2 Sew the blocks together into rows, and then join the rows. The quilt center should measure 11" square, including seam allowances.

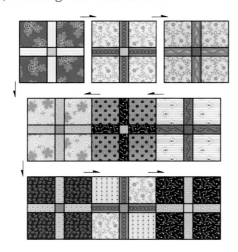

Finishing the Quilt

For help with the following finishing steps, go to ShopMartingale.com/HowtoQuilt for free, illustrated instructions.

1 Layer and baste the quilt top, batting, and backing. Quilt by hand or machine. The quilt shown is quilted with an X in each block, and in-the-ditch quilting is added around the quilt center. Diagonal lines are quilted 1" apart in the outer border.

2 Using the red 1¼"-wide strips, prepare and attach single-fold binding (which some designers prefer to double-fold binding for small quilts).

3 Add a hanging sleeve, if desired.

Susan's Courage

Quilts are often made as heartfelt gifts, but they can also be loving tributes—in this case, to a dear friend who showed grace and courage in the face of illness. Selecting a dark print for the setting pieces allows the blocks and border to shine.

Finished quilt: 22½" × 28⅛"
Finished block: 4" × 4"

Designed and made by Carol Hopkins

Materials

Yardage is based on 42"-wide fabric.

⅓ yard of light print for blocks

12 scraps, at least 5" × 5" each, of assorted dark prints for blocks

12 scraps, at least 4" × 4" each, of assorted medium prints for blocks

½ yard of dark purple print for setting squares and triangles

1 yard of floral stripe OR ½ yard of nondirectional floral print for border

⅓ yard of light purple print for binding

1 yard of fabric for backing

31" × 36" piece of batting

Cutting

All measurements include ¼"-wide seam allowances.

From the light print, cut:

3 strips, 1⅞" × 42"; crosscut into 48 squares, 1⅞" × 1⅞". Cut in half diagonally to yield 96 triangles.

2 strips, 1½" × 42"; crosscut into 48 squares, 1½" × 1½"

From *each* of the dark scraps, cut:

4 squares, 1⅞" × 1⅞"; cut in half diagonally to yield 8 triangles (96 total)

From *each* of the medium scraps, cut:

4 squares, 1½" × 1½" (48 total)

From the dark purple print, cut:

1 strip, 7" × 42"; crosscut into:

- 3 squares, 7" × 7"; cut into quarters diagonally to yield 12 side triangles (2 are extra)
- 2 squares, 3¾" × 3¾"; cut in half diagonally to yield 4 corner triangles

1 strip, 4½" × 42"; crosscut into 6 squares, 4½" × 4½"

From the *lengthwise* grain of the floral stripe, cut*:

4 strips, 3" × 36"

From the light purple print, cut:

4 strips, 2" × 42"

*If you're using a nondirectional print, cut the strips across the fabric width.

Making the Blocks

One dark and one medium print are used in each block. Press all seam allowances as indicated by the arrows or as otherwise specified.

1 Sew a dark 1⅞" triangle to a light 1⅞" triangle to make a half-square-triangle unit. Make eight matching units measuring 1½" square.

Make 8.

2 Sew the blocks, setting squares, and side triangles together in diagonal rows; press.

3 Sew the rows together, pressing the seam allowances open after adding each row. Add the corner triangles; press.

Quilt assembly

4 Trim the quilt top if necessary, leaving a ¼" seam allowance beyond the points of the blocks.

5 Measure the length of the quilt top through the center and trim two of the floral strips to this measurement. Sew the strips to the sides of the quilt.

6 Measure the width of the quilt top through the center, including the just-added border pieces, and trim the two remaining floral strips to this

2 Arrange the half-square-triangle units, four medium 1½" squares, and four light 1½" squares as shown. Sew the pieces into rows. Sew the rows together to make a block measuring 4½" square. Make 12 blocks.

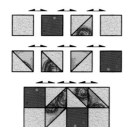 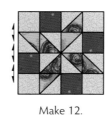

Make 12.

Assembling the Quilt Top

1 Arrange the blocks and dark purple 4½" squares in diagonal rows as shown below. Add the purple 7" side triangles and 3¾" corner triangles.

measurement. Sew the strips to the top and bottom of the quilt.

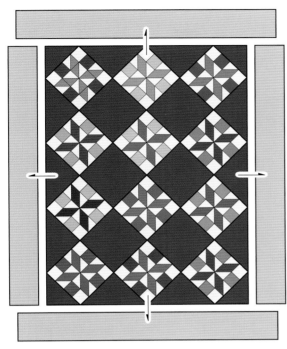

Adding borders

Finishing the Quilt

For help with the following finishing steps, go to ShopMartingale.com/HowtoQuilt for free, illustrated instructions.

1 Layer and baste the quilt top, batting, and backing. Quilt by hand or machine.

2 Using the light purple 2"-wide strips, prepare and attach double-fold binding.

3 Add a hanging sleeve, if desired.

Opposition

The Civil War era is fertile ground when longtime quiltmaking partners Mary and Connie are looking for inspiration. The tiny triangle squares surrounding Sawtooth Stars symbolize troops protecting their land, their homes, and all they hold dear.

Finished quilt: 30½" × 30½"
Finished block: 6" × 6"

Designed and made by Mary Etherington and Connie Tesene

Materials

Yardage is based on 42"-wide fabric.

⅛ yard *each* of 39 assorted light, medium, and dark prints for blocks and pieced border
⅝ yard of green print for setting triangles and inner border
⅓ yard of blue print for binding
1 yard of fabric for backing
34" × 34" piece of batting

Cutting

All measurements include ¼"-wide seam allowances.

CUTTING FOR 1 STAR BLOCK

Cut 13 blocks total.

From *1* of the assorted prints, cut:
1 square, 2½" × 2½"
8 squares, 1½" × 1½"

From *1* of the assorted prints, cut:
4 rectangles, 1½" × 2½"
4 squares, 1½" × 1½"

From *1* of the dark prints, cut:
8 squares, 1⅞" × 1⅞"; cut in half diagonally to yield 16 triangles
2 squares, 1½" × 1½"

From *1* of the light prints, cut:
8 squares, 1⅞" × 1⅞"; cut in half diagonally to yield 16 triangles
2 squares, 1½" × 1½"

CUTTING FOR SETTING TRIANGLES AND INNER BORDER

From the green print, cut:
2 squares, 10¾" × 10¾"; cut into quarters diagonally to yield 8 side triangles*
2 squares, 6½" × 6½"; cut in half diagonally to yield 4 corner triangles*
2 strips, 1¼" × 26"
2 strips, 1¼" × 27½"

*The side and corner triangles are cut slightly oversized and will be trimmed later.

Continued on page 112

Continued from page 111

CUTTING FOR PIECED BORDER AND BINDING

From the assorted dark prints, cut:

36 squares, 2⅜" × 2⅜"; cut in half diagonally to yield 72 triangles

From the assorted light prints, cut:

36 squares, 2⅜" × 2⅜"; cut in half diagonally to yield 72 triangles

From the assorted medium prints, cut:

4 squares, 2" × 2"

From the blue print, cut:

4 strips, 2¼" × 42"

Making the Blocks

For each center star unit, select one print for the star and a contrasting print for the background. Press all seam allowances as indicated by the arrows or as otherwise specified.

1 Draw a diagonal line on the wrong side of eight star 1½" squares. Place a marked square on a background 1½" × 2½" rectangle, right sides together. Sew on the drawn line. Trim the outside corner of the square only, ¼" from the stitched line. Press toward the corner. Repeat on the other end of the rectangle. Make four units.

Make 4.

2 Join the four units from step 1, four background 1½" squares, and one star 2½" square in rows. The block should measure 4½" square.

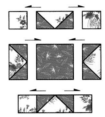

3 Sew 16 matching light 1⅞" triangles to 16 matching dark 1⅞" triangles to make 16 half-square-triangle units.

Make 16.

4 Join the center star unit, the half-square-triangle units, two light 1½" squares that match the triangle units, and two dark 1½" squares that match the triangle units. Make 13 blocks.

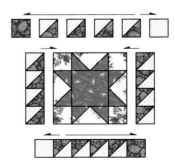 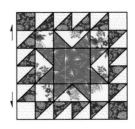

Make 13.

Assembling the Quilt Top

1 Sew a pair of light and dark 2⅜" triangles together. Press the seam allowances toward the dark triangle. Make 72 units.

2 Sew 18 half-square-triangle units together, orienting the dark triangles in the same direction. Make four border strips.

Make 4.

3 Sew a medium 2" square to each end of a border strip from step 2 to make a side border strip. Make two side borders.

Make 2.

4 Arrange the blocks and the green side and corner triangles in diagonal rows as shown. Sew the blocks and side triangles into rows. Join the rows, pressing the seam allowances open, and add the corner triangles last. Trim the oversized triangles all around, leaving an equal amount from the block corners so that the quilt top measures 26" × 26". You'll need this size to be accurate for the pieced triangle border to fit properly.

Quilt assembly

5 Sew the green 1¼" × 26" strips to the top and bottom of the quilt top. Sew the green 1¼" × 27½" strips to the quilt sides.

6 Sew the 18-unit border strips from step 2 to the top and bottom of the quilt top. Sew the border strips from step 3 to the quilt sides.

Quilt plan

Finishing the Quilt

For help with the following finishing steps, go to ShopMartingale.com/HowtoQuilt for free, illustrated instructions.

1 Layer and baste the quilt top, batting, and backing. Quilt by hand or machine.

2 Using the blue 2¼"-wide strips, prepare and attach double-fold binding.

3 Add a hanging sleeve, if desired.

Redware and Harvest

Rich brown tones, madder reds, and cheerful cheddar evoke the magic of fall, but don't keep this quilt hidden away until harvest season rolls around. The double dose of triangles in the Pinwheel blocks provide a delightful accent year-round.

Finished quilt: 28¼" × 28¼"
Finished block: 7½" × 7½"

Designed and made by Jo Morton

Materials

Yardage is based on 42"-wide fabric. Fat quarters are 18" × 21".

Scraps (about ¼ yard *total*) of assorted light prints for blocks

Scraps (about ½ yard *total*) of assorted brown and rust prints for blocks

1 fat quarter of cheddar print for blocks

1 fat quarter of rust print for setting triangles

¾ yard of tan print for inner border and cornerstones

¾ yard of dark brown print for outer border

1 fat quarter OR ¼ yard of rust plaid for single-fold binding

1 yard of fabric for backing

33" × 33" piece of batting

Cutting

All measurements include ¼"-wide seam allowances.

From the scraps of light prints, cut a *total* of:
30 squares, 2¼" × 2¼"

From the scraps of brown and rust prints, cut a *total* of:
60 squares, 2¼" × 2¼"; cut 30 of the squares in half diagonally to yield 60 triangles

From the cheddar print, cut:
10 squares, 5" × 5"

From the rust print for setting triangles, cut:
1 square, 12½" × 12½"; cut into quarters diagonally to yield 4 side triangles
2 squares, 6½" × 6½"; cut in half diagonally to yield 4 corner triangles

From the *lengthwise* grain of the tan print, cut:*
2 strips, 1¾" × 24¼"
2 strips, 1¾" × 21¾"
4 squares, 2½" × 2½"

From the *lengthwise* grain of the dark brown print, cut:*
4 strips, 2½" × 24¼"

From the rust plaid, cut:
1⅛"-wide bias strips totaling at least 125" when joined

*Jo recommends cutting these pieces on the lengthwise grain of the fabric (parallel to the selvage) because it has the least amount of stretch and will give you nice, straight edges.

Making the Blocks

Use a scant ¼" seam allowance throughout. Press the seam allowances as indicated by the arrows. At seam intersections, cut through both layers of the seam allowance, right up to but not through the stitching. This will allow you to press the clipped intersections open.

1 Draw a diagonal line from corner to corner on the wrong side of each light square. Lay a marked square on top of a brown or rust square, right sides together. Sew a scant ¼" from each side of the drawn line. Cut the unit apart on the drawn line to make two half-square-triangle units. Trim each unit to measure 1¾" square. Make a total of 60 units.

Make 60.

2 Lay out three half-square-triangle units and three brown or rust triangles as shown. Sew the units and triangles together into rows. Pin and sew the rows together, matching the seam intersections. Make 20 units.

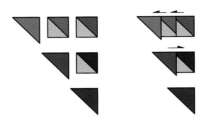

Make 20.

3 Place two units on top of a cheddar 5" square, right sides together. Using the edge of each unit as a guide, sew using a full ¼" seam allowance, making sure the seamline is just outside the light triangle points. (In other words, you'll need to sew wider than a scant ¼" seam allowance here.) Cut the unit apart as shown. Press and trim the units to measure 4¼" square. Make 20 units.

Make 20.

4 Join four units as shown to form a Pinwheel block measuring 8" square, including seam allowances. Make five blocks.

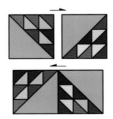 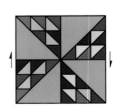

Make 5.

Assembling the Quilt Top

1 Lay out the Pinwheel blocks, rust side triangles, and corner triangles in diagonal rows. Join the pieces in rows. Sew the rows together, matching the seam intersections. Add the corner triangles last. Square up the quilt top to measure 21¾" square, including seam allowances, making sure to leave a ¼" seam allowance beyond all points.

Quilt assembly

2 Sew the tan 1¾" × 21¾" strips to opposite sides of the quilt top. Sew the tan 1¾" × 24¼" strips to the top and bottom of the quilt top.

3 Sew dark brown 2½" × 24¼" strips to opposite sides of the quilt top. Sew a tan 2½" square to each end of the remaining dark brown strips. Sew these strips to the top and bottom of the quilt top.

Finishing the Quilt

For help with the following finishing steps, go to ShopMartingale.com/HowtoQuilt for free, illustrated instructions.

1 Layer and baste the quilt top, batting, and backing. Quilt by hand or machine. The quilt shown is machine quilted in a crosshatch grid across the quilt from edge to edge, following the diagonal line spacing created by the patchwork.

2 Using the rust plaid 1⅛"-wide bias strips, prepare and attach single-fold binding (which some designers prefer to double-fold binding for small quilts).

3 Add a hanging sleeve, if desired.

Bonnet Ties

Tiny squares flow diagonally across this quilt like the long ribbon ties that secured fancy bonnets worn by nineteenth-century women. For added interest, include large-scale prints when choosing your assorted medium and dark scraps for Pinwheel blocks.

Finished quilt: 27" × 33"
Finished block: 3" × 3"

*Designed and pieced by Carol Hopkins;
quilted by Lisa Ramsey*

Materials

Yardage is based on 42"-wide fabric.

32 assorted medium print scraps, at least 6" × 6", for Pinwheel blocks

32 assorted dark print scraps, at least 6" × 6", for Pinwheel blocks

124 assorted dark print scraps, at least 1½" × 1½", for Double Four Patch blocks

⅝ yard of light print for Double Four Patch blocks

1⅛ yards of blue stripe OR ¾ yard of nondirectional blue print for border

⅜ yard of blue print for binding

1 yard of fabric for backing

33" × 39" piece of batting

Cutting

All measurements include ¼"-wide seam allowances.

From *each* of the medium scraps, cut:
2 squares, 2⅜" × 2⅜"; cut in half diagonally to yield 4 triangles (128 total)

From *each* of the dark 6" × 6" scraps, cut:
2 squares, 2⅜" × 2⅜"; cut in half diagonally to yield 4 triangles (128 total)

From *each* of the dark 1½" × 1½" scraps, cut:
1 square, 1¼" × 1¼" (124 total)

From the light print, cut:
62 squares, 2" × 2"
124 squares, 1¼" × 1¼"

From the *lengthwise* grain of the blue stripe, cut:*
4 strips, 3½" × 40"

From the blue print, cut:
4 strips, 2" × 40"

*If you are using a nondirectional print, cut the strips across the fabric width.

Making the Pinwheel Blocks

Press all seam allowances as indicated by the arrows or as otherwise specified.

1 For each Pinwheel block, select four matching medium triangles and four matching dark triangles. Sew a medium triangle to a dark triangle. Make four matching half-square-triangle units.

Make 4.

two units measuring 2" square, including seam allowances.

Make 2.

2 Arrange the units from step 1 and two light 2" squares as shown. Sew the pieces together into rows. Sew the rows together to complete the block. Make 31 Double Four Patch blocks measuring 3½" square, including seam allowances.

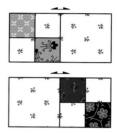 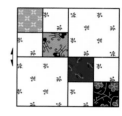

Make 31.

Assembling the Quilt Top

1 Arrange the Pinwheel blocks and Double Four Patch blocks into nine rows of seven blocks each as shown. Sew the blocks together into rows. Sew the rows together.

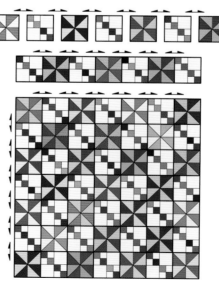

Quilt assembly

2 Arrange the four units as shown. Sew the units together into rows, and then sew the rows together to complete the block. Make 32 Pinwheel blocks measuring 3½" square, including seam allowances.

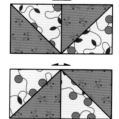 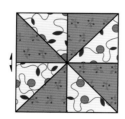

Make 32.

Making the Double Four Patch Blocks

The light print is paired with four different dark prints in each of the blocks.

1 Sew two light 1¼" squares and two different dark 1¼" squares together to make a four patch. Make

2 Measure the length of the quilt through the center and add 8". Trim two blue-striped 3½"-wide strips to this measurement. Pin the strips to the sides of the quilt, right sides together, matching the centers. Sew these strips to the quilt. (Visit ShopMartingale.com/HowtoQuilt if you would like illustrated instructions about adding a mitered border.)

3 Measure the quilt width, without the border, and add 8". Trim the two remaining blue-striped strips to this measurement. Center and pin these strips to the top and bottom of the quilt, right sides together. Sew these strips to the quilt.

4 Miter the border at each corner of the quilt.

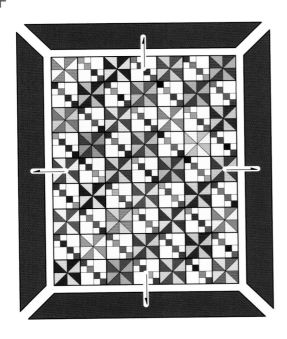

Finishing the Quilt

For help with the following finishing steps, go to ShopMartingale.com/HowtoQuilt for free, illustrated instructions.

1 Layer and baste the quilt top, batting, and backing. Quilt by hand or machine.

2 Using the blue print 2"-wide strips, prepare and attach double-fold binding.

3 Add a hanging sleeve, if desired.

Optional Border with Butted Corners

If you have chosen a nondirectional border print, you may prefer not to miter the quilt border. Follow these instructions instead.

1 Measure the length of the quilt top through the center and trim two blue strips to this measurement. Sew the strips to the sides of the quilt and press the seam allowances toward the border.

2 Measure the width of the quilt top through the center, including the just-added border pieces, and trim the two remaining blue strips to this measurement. Sew the strips to the top and bottom of the quilt and press the seam allowances toward the border.

Joyful Jumble

If you love creating quilts with a make-do, not-too-perfect appeal, this patchwork design's for you. For ease, the instructions are written so that each block features matching prints, but feel free to mix things up to make your own joyful jumble!

Finished quilt: 18½" × 24½"
Finished block: 3" × 3"

Designed and made by Sheryl Johnson

Materials

Yardage is based on 42"-wide fabric.

½ yard *total* of assorted light, medium, and dark print scraps in reds, browns, grays, creams, blues, and greens for blocks

½ yard of light solid for blocks

¼ yard of brown print for single-fold binding

⅔ yard of fabric for backing

23" × 28" piece of cream flannel or batting

Cutting

All measurements include ¼"-wide seam allowances.

From the assorted light, medium, and dark prints, cut 48 matching sets of:

1 square, 2½" × 2½" (48 total)
2 squares, 2" × 2" (96 total)

From the light solid, cut:

2 strips, 1½" × 42"; crosscut into 48 squares, 1½" × 1½"
5 strips, 2" × 42"; crosscut into 96 squares, 2" × 2"

From the brown print, cut:

3 strips, 1½" × 42"

Making the Blocks

Press all seam allowances as indicated by the arrows.

1 Draw a diagonal line from corner to corner on the wrong side of a light solid 2" square and layer it on top of a print 2" square, right sides together. Sew ¼" from both sides of the drawn line. Cut on the line to yield two half-square-triangle units. Trim the units to 1½" square, including seam allowances. Make 192 units.

Make 192 units,
1½" × 1½".

2 Organize groups of four matching half-square-triangle units, one group for each of the 48 blocks.

3 Arrange one dark 2½" square, one light solid 1½" square, and four half-square-triangle units as shown on page 124, noting the orientation of the half-square triangles. Join the half-square-triangle units. Join the light square to the horizontal row of half-square triangles, and join the dark square to the

to row. The rows should measure 3½" × 18½", including seam allowances.

Make 8 rows,
3½" × 18½".

3 Sew the eight rows together as shown, matching the seams at the block intersections. The completed quilt top should measure 18½" × 24½".

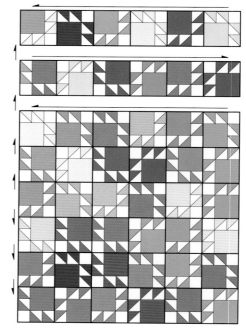

Quilt assembly

vertical row of half-square triangles. Join the two rows to complete one block, which should measure 3½" square, including seam allowances. Make 48 blocks.

Make 48 blocks,
3½" × 3½".

Assembling the Quilt Top

1 Referring to the quilt assembly diagram at right, arrange the blocks in eight rows of six blocks each. For the Joyful Jumble layout, the large print square in each block alternates from row to row, shifting from the upper-left to lower-left corner and from the upper-right to lower-right corner. There are a few exceptions, however; feel free to match the layout exactly, or rotate the blocks as desired.

2 Join the blocks in rows. Press the seam allowances in opposite directions from row

Finishing the Quilt

For help with the following finishing steps, go to ShopMartingale.com/HowtoQuilt for free, illustrated instructions.

1 Layer and baste the quilt top, batting, and backing. Quilt by hand or machine. The quilt shown is hand quilted diagonally through the unpieced squares in each block.

2 Using the brown print 1½"-wide strips, prepare and attach single-fold binding (which some designers prefer to double-fold binding for small quilts).

3 Add a hanging sleeve, if desired.

President's Pride

If you've never tried your hand at a medallion quilt, this is a great opportunity. It's not too big, and most of the blocks are quite easy. Notice, in addition, that a plain border separates each round, giving you the chance to square up the quilt between rounds.

Finished quilt: 36½" × 36½"
Finished blocks: 12" × 12", 3" × 3",
and 4½" × 4½"

*Designed and made by Mary Etherington
and Connie Tesene*

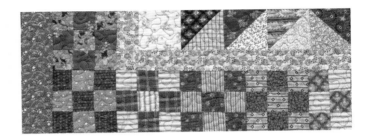

Materials

Yardage is based on 42"-wide fabric.

⅛ yard *each* of 15 assorted light prints for blocks
    and triangle border
⅛ yard *each* of 15 assorted dark prints for blocks
⅛ yard *each* of 6 assorted red prints for blocks and
    triangle border
⅛ yard of beige print for Triangle Square Star block
⅛ yard of medium blue print for border 2
⅓ yard of dark blue print for border 4
⅓ yard of brown print for binding
1 yard of fabric for backing
40" × 40" piece of batting

Cutting

All measurements include ¼"-wide seam allowances.

CUTTING FOR THE TRIANGLE
SQUARE STAR BLOCK

From *each* of 8 dark prints, cut:
1 square, 3⅞" × 3⅞" (8 total); cut in half diagonally
    to yield 2 triangles (16 total)

From the beige print, cut:
4 squares, 3⅞" × 3⅞"; cut in half diagonally to yield
    8 triangles
4 squares, 3½" × 3½"

CUTTING FOR THE TRIANGLE BORDER

From the assorted red prints, cut:
12 squares, 2⅞" × 2⅞"; cut in half diagonally to yield
    24 triangles

From the assorted light prints, cut:
12 squares, 2⅞" × 2⅞"; cut in half diagonally to yield
    24 triangles

From *1* of the light prints, cut:
4 squares, 2½" × 2½"

CUTTING FOR 1 NINE PATCH BLOCK

Cut 28 blocks total.

From *1* of the assorted dark prints, cut:
5 squares, 1½" × 1½"
4 matching squares, 1½" × 1½"

From *1* of the assorted light prints, cut:
5 matching squares, 1½" × 1½"
4 matching squares, 1½" × 1½"

Continued on page 126

Making the Triangle Square Star Block

Press all seam allowances as indicated by the arrows or as otherwise specified.

1 Sew a beige triangle to a dark 3⅞" triangle to make a half-square-triangle unit. Make eight units.

Make 8.

2 Repeat step 1, sewing two different dark 3⅞" triangles together. Press the seam allowances toward the darker triangle. Make four units.

3 Arrange the beige 3½" squares and the units from steps 1 and 2 in four rows as shown, making sure to position units so that the dark triangles form eight star points. Sew the pieces together into rows. Sew the rows together. The block should measure 12½" square, including seam allowances.

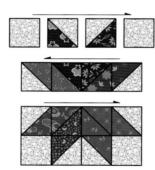 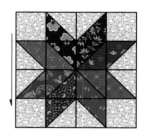

Make 1.

Making the Triangle Border

1 Sew a light 2⅞" triangle to a red 2⅞" triangle to make a half-square-triangle unit. Press the seam allowances toward the red triangle. The unit should measure 2½" square, including seam allowances. Make 24 units.

2 Sew six units from step 1 together, orienting the dark triangles as shown on page 128. Make two

Continued from page 125

CUTTING FOR 1 SHOOFLY BLOCK

Cut 28 blocks total. The "shoofly" can be darker or lighter than the background, so the fabrics are listed as "background" and "shoofly." You'll need 28 background fabrics and 28 shoofly fabrics. Refer to the photo above for guidance with fabric placement as needed.

From *1* of the background fabrics, cut:
2 squares, 2⅜" × 2⅜"; cut in half diagonally to yield 4 triangles
4 squares, 2" × 2"

From *1* of the shoofly fabrics, cut:
2 squares, 2⅜" × 2⅜"; cut in half diagonally to yield 4 triangles
1 square, 2" × 2"

CUTTING FOR BORDERS AND BINDING

From the medium blue print, cut:
2 strips, 1½" × 16½"
2 strips, 1½" × 18½"

From the dark blue print, cut:
2 strips, 2" × 24½"
2 strips, 2" × 27½"

From the brown print, cut:
4 strips, 2¼" × 42"

borders for the top and bottom of the quilt center. For the side borders, sew six units together in the same manner, and join a light 2½" square to each end. Make two borders.

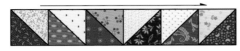

Make 2.

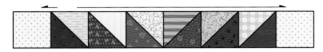

Make 2.

Making the Nine Patch Blocks

Select five matching dark 1½" squares and four matching light 1½" squares. Sew the squares together into rows. Sew the rows together to make a Nine Patch block. The block should measure 3½" square. Make 14 blocks.

Make 14.

Making the Reverse Nine Patch Blocks

Select five matching light 1½" squares and four matching dark 1½" squares. Sew the squares together into rows. Sew the rows together to make a reverse Nine Patch block. The block should measure 3½" square. Make 14 blocks.

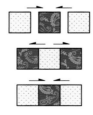

Make 14.

Making the Shoofly Blocks

Use one shoofly fabric and one background fabric for each block. Refer to the quilt photo for help with fabric placement as needed.

1 Sew a shoofly 2⅜" triangle to a background 2⅜" triangle to make a half-square-triangle unit. Press the seam allowances toward the darker triangle. The unit should measure 2" square. Make four units.

2 Arrange the half-square-triangle units, four background 2" squares, and one shoofly 2" square in three rows. Sew the pieces together into rows. Sew the rows together. The block should measure 5" square. Make 28 blocks.

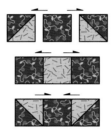

Make 28.

Assembling the Quilt Top

1 Sew the triangle borders to the top, bottom, and sides of the Triangle Square Star block. The quilt-top center should measure 16½" square.

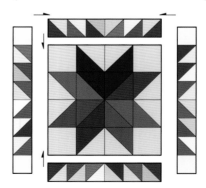

2 Sew the medium blue 1½" × 16½" strips to the top and bottom of the quilt-top center. Sew the medium blue 1½" × 18½" strips to the sides of the quilt top.

3 Sew three Nine Patch blocks and three reverse Nine Patch blocks together to make a border strip. Make two borders for the top and bottom of the quilt. Sew four Nine Patch blocks and four reverse Nine Patch blocks together to make a border strip. Make two for the side borders.

Make 2.

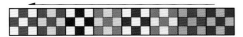

Make 2.

4 Sew the Nine Patch borders to the top, bottom, and sides of the quilt top. The quilt-top center should measure 24½" square.

5 Sew the dark blue 2" × 24½" strips to the top and bottom of the quilt-top center. Sew the dark blue 2" × 27½" strips to the sides of the quilt top.

6 Sew six Shoofly blocks together to make a border strip. Make two borders for the top and bottom of the quilt. Sew eight Shoofly blocks together to make a border strip. Make two for the side borders.

Make 2.

Make 2.

7 Sew the Shoofly borders to the top, bottom, and sides of the quilt top.

Quilt assembly

Finishing the Quilt

For help with the following finishing steps, go to ShopMartingale.com/HowtoQuilt for free, illustrated instructions.

1 Layer and baste the quilt top, batting, and backing. Quilt by hand or machine.

2 Using the brown 2¼"-wide strips, prepare and attach double-fold binding.

3 Add a hanging sleeve, if desired.

Courthouse Steps

It's not surprising that so many quiltmakers love Courthouse Steps blocks; the way the fabrics are placed can make the blocks seem very different from one another, so the possibilities are endless. For this design, Jo recommends sticking with a limited palette.

Finished quilt: 15½" × 20½"
Finished block: 5" × 5"

Designed and made by Jo Morton

Materials

Yardage is based on 42"-wide fabric. Fat quarters are 18" × 21"; fat eighths are 9" × 21".

16 fat eighths of assorted navy prints for blocks
15 fat eighths of assorted brown prints for blocks
1 fat eighth of rust print for blocks
1 fat quarter OR ¼ yard of red print for single-fold binding
⅝ yard of fabric for backing
20" × 25" piece of batting

Cutting

All measurements include ¼"-wide seam allowances.

From the *lengthwise* grain of each navy print, cut:*
8 strips, 1" × 9" (128 total; you'll use 96, but cutting extra allows for more fabric variety)

From the *lengthwise* grain of each brown print, cut:*
8 strips, 1" × 9" (120 total; you'll use 96, but cutting extra allows for more fabric variety)

From the rust print, cut:
12 squares, 1½" × 1½"

From the red print, cut:
5 strips, 1⅛" × 21"

*Jo recommends cutting these pieces on the lengthwise grain (parallel to the selvage) because it has the least amount of stretch and results in a nice, flat quilt top.

Planning Your Color Scheme

To make planning easier, first decide on your palette. Then cut 4" squares of your chosen colors. Arrange the squares on point on your design wall; fold the side squares in half to create side triangles. When you like the fabric placement, take a photo of your color plan for reference and cut the 1" strips needed for your blocks. Notice in the quilt shown on page 132 that four fabrics are used in each block plus a rust square in the center. The adjoining blocks share the same fabric, so pay attention to the fabric sequence.

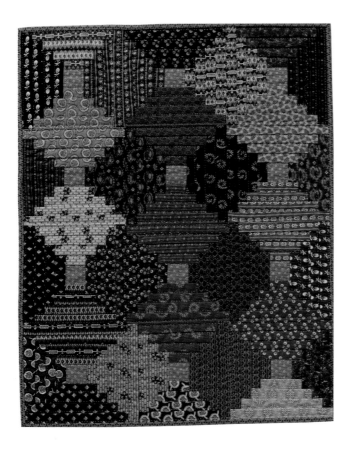

Making the Blocks

To make a Courthouse Steps block, add strips to opposite sides of a center square first and then to the two remaining sides. In block A, join the vertical strips to the center square first. In block B, sew the horizontal strips to the center square first. (The numbers in the illustrations show the sewing order.) This makes assembling the quilt top easier.

Use a scant ¼" seam allowance throughout. Press all seam allowances away from the center square.

1 Using the strips from two navy prints, label them fabrics W and X. Using the strips from two brown prints, label them fabrics Y and Z.

2 Sew a rust 1½" square to a fabric W strip, right sides together, with the square on top. Press. Trim the ends of the strip even with the rust square.

3 In the same way, sew a fabric X strip to the opposite side of the rust square. Press and trim as before.

4 Sew a fabric Y strip to the top edge of the unit. Press and trim as before. Sew a fabric Z strip to the bottom edge of the unit. Press and trim. You have now added one round of strips to the center square. Square the unit to measure 2½" square. *Note:* When pressing, be careful that you don't distort the unit. Measure the unit after adding, and press each round of strips to keep the block accurate. Each complete round of strips will add 1" to the measurement.

5 Continue adding strips in sequence to opposite sides of the unit (as indicated by the numbers in the block illustration) to make block A. Sew, press, and trim each strip as before. The block should measure 5½" square. Make a total of six A blocks.

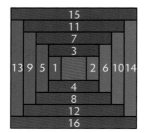

Block A.
Make 6.

6 To make a B block, sew a rust 1½" square to a fabric Y strip, right sides together, with the square on top. Press and trim. Sew a fabric Z strip to the opposite side of the rust square. Press and trim.

7 Sew a fabric W strip to the left edge of the unit. Press and trim as before. Sew a fabric X strip to the right edge of the unit. Press and trim. You have

now added one round of strips to the center square. Square the unit to measure 2½" square.

8 Continue adding strips in numerical order to make block B. Sew, press, and trim each strip as before. The block should measure 5½" square. Make a total of six B blocks.

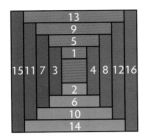

Block B.
Make 6.

Assembling the Quilt Top

Use a scant ¼" seam allowance throughout. Press all seam allowances open to reduce bulk.

1 Lay out your blocks in four rows of three blocks each, making sure to rotate the blocks so adjoining blocks have the same fabrics.

2 Sew the blocks together into rows, and then join the rows.

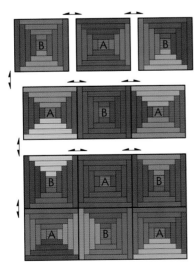

Quilt assembly

Finishing the Quilt

For help with the following finishing steps, go to ShopMartingale.com/HowtoQuilt for free, illustrated instructions.

1 Layer and baste the quilt top, batting, and backing. Quilt by hand or machine. The quilt shown is hand quilted with tan thread approximately ¹⁄₁₆" to ⅛" from the ditch. This creates two lines of quilting, approximately ³⁄₁₆" apart, where the blocks are joined.

2 Using the red 1⅛"-wide strips, prepare and attach single-fold binding (which some designers prefer to double-fold binding for small quilts).

3 Add a hanging sleeve, if desired.

Allie Beane

Scrappy and happy and chock-full of fun prints, this is a great quilt for making a dent in your stash. To help the pinwheel center stand out, select a color that contrasts well with the dark squares in the block.

Finished quilt: 31¾" × 37¼"
Finished block: 4¼" × 4¼"

Designed and pieced by Carol Hopkins; quilted by Lisa Ramsey

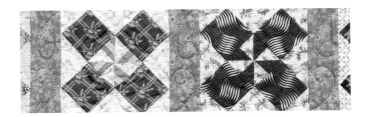

Materials

Yardage is based on 42"-wide fabric.

20 assorted light print scraps, at least 6" × 6", for blocks

20 assorted medium or dark print scraps, at least 2" × 4", for blocks

20 assorted medium or dark print scraps, at least 5" × 5", for blocks

½ yard of gold print for sashing

¼ yard of tan print for cornerstones

¼ yard of red print for inner border

¾ yard of brown floral for outer border and binding

1¼ yards of fabric for backing

38" × 44" piece of batting

Cutting

All measurements include ¼"-wide seam allowances.

From *each* of the light scraps, cut:

1 square, 3⅜" × 3⅜"; cut into quarters diagonally to yield 4 triangles (80 total)

2 squares, 2" × 2"; cut in half diagonally to yield 4 triangles (80 total)

2 squares, 1⅝" × 1⅝"; cut in half diagonally to yield 4 triangles (80 total)

From *each* of the medium or dark 2" × 4" scraps, cut:

2 squares, 1⅝" × 1⅝"; cut in half diagonally to yield 4 triangles (80 total)

From *each* of the medium or dark 5" × 5" scraps, cut:

4 squares, 2" × 2" (80 total)

From the gold print, cut:

49 rectangles, 1¾" × 4¾"

From the tan print, cut:

30 squares, 1¾" × 1¾"

From the red print, cut:

4 strips, 1½" × 42"

From the brown floral, cut:

4 strips, 3¾" × 42"

4 strips, 2" × 42"

Making the Blocks

A light print is paired with two different medium or dark prints in each of the blocks. Press all seam allowances as indicated by the arrows.

1 Sew a light 1⅝" triangle to a medium or dark 1⅝" triangle to make a half-square-triangle unit. Make four matching units measuring 1¼" square.

Make 4.

4 Sew a matching light 2" triangle to each corner of the unit. Leaving ¼" for seam allowance on all sides of the block, trim the excess triangle fabric so that the block measures 4¾" square. Make 20 blocks.

Make 20.

Assembling the Quilt Top

1 Arrange the blocks, sashing rectangles, and cornerstones as shown. Sew the pieces together into rows. Sew the rows together.

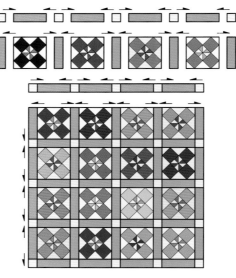

Quilt assembly

2 Arrange the units as shown. Sew them together into rows, and then sew the rows together to make a pinwheel measuring 2" square.

Make 1.

3 Arrange the pinwheel, four matching medium or dark 2" squares, and four light 3⅜" triangles that match the light fabric in the pinwheel. Sew the pieces together into diagonal rows and then sew the rows together.

 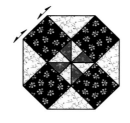

2 For the inner border, measure the length of the quilt top through the center and trim two of the red strips to this measurement. Sew the strips to the sides of the quilt.

3 Measure the width of the quilt top through the center, including the just-added border pieces, and trim the two remaining red strips to this measurement. Sew the strips to the top and bottom of the quilt.

4 For the outer border, measure the length of the quilt top through the center and trim two of the brown 3¾"-wide strips to this measurement. Sew the strips to the sides of the quilt.

5 Measure the width of the quilt top through the center, including the just-added border pieces, and trim the two remaining brown 3¾"-wide strips to this measurement. Sew the strips to the top and bottom of the quilt.

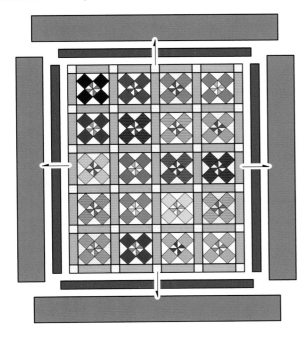

Finishing the Quilt

For help with the following finishing steps, go to ShopMartingale.com/HowtoQuilt for free, illustrated instructions.

1 Layer and baste the quilt top, batting, and backing. Quilt by hand or machine.

2 Using the brown 2"-wide strips, prepare and attach double-fold binding.

3 Add a hanging sleeve, if desired.

June Bug

Strawberry prints and striped binding? Yes, please! Charmingly cheerful in every way, this mini features simple strip-pieced blocks and orange-peel appliqués. You'll save time by using precut 5" squares for the blocks—and use them for the backing too, if you like!

Finished quilt: 15½" × 15½"
Finished block: 4" × 4"

Designed and made by Camille Roskelley

Materials

Fat quarters are 18" × 21".

11 squares, 5" × 5", of assorted prints for blocks*
1 fat quarter of white solid for blocks
1 fat quarter of aqua print for border
1 fat quarter of diagonal stripe for binding
1 fat quarter of fabric for backing**
18" × 18" piece of batting
⅓ yard of 18"-wide lightweight fusible web

Precut charm squares (5" × 5") work perfectly for this project.
**As an alternative, Camille suggests using 16 charm squares to make a pieced backing.*

Cutting

All measurements include ¼"-wide seam allowances.

From the white solid, cut:
5 squares, 4½" × 4½"

From 6 of the assorted-print squares, cut a *total* of:
16 strips, 1½" × 4½"

From the aqua print, cut:
2 strips, 2" × 12½"
2 strips, 2" × 15½"

From the diagonal stripe, cut:
4 strips, 2" × 21"

Making the Blocks

Press all seam allowances as indicated by the arrows. If you need more information, you can download free instructions about appliqué and embroidery stitches at ShopMartingale.com/HowtoQuilt.

1 Trace the complete pattern for the orange peel (four petals plus the outer square) on page 141 onto the paper side of fusible web. Make five traced patterns and cut them out on the lines of the square.

2 Following the manufacturer's instructions, fuse one square to the wrong side of each of the five uncut 5" squares, centering the fusible web on the fabric square. Cut each petal out along the lines, leaving the rest of the fused square intact. Remove the paper backing and set aside.

Assembling the Quilt Top

1 Lay out three rows of three blocks each, alternating the blocks as shown below. Join the blocks in each row. Join the rows.

2 Sew the aqua 2" × 12½" strips to the sides of the quilt. Sew the aqua 2" × 15½" strips to the top and bottom of the quilt.

Quilt assembly

3 Arrange four matching petals on a white 4½" square using the fusible-web paper from step 2 as a guide for placement. Fuse the petals in place and blanket-stitch the edge of each petal by hand or machine. Make five appliquéd blocks.

Make 5.

Finishing the Quilt

For help with the following finishing steps, go to ShopMartingale.com/HowtoQuilt for free, illustrated instructions.

1 Layer and baste the quilt top, batting, and backing. Quilt by hand or machine. The quilt shown is machine quilted with parallel straight lines.

2 Using the diagonal stripe 2"-wide strips, prepare and attach double-fold binding.

3 Add a hanging sleeve, if desired.

4 Sew four assorted print 1½" × 4½" strips together to make a block measuring 4½" square. Make four pieced blocks.

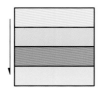

Make 4.

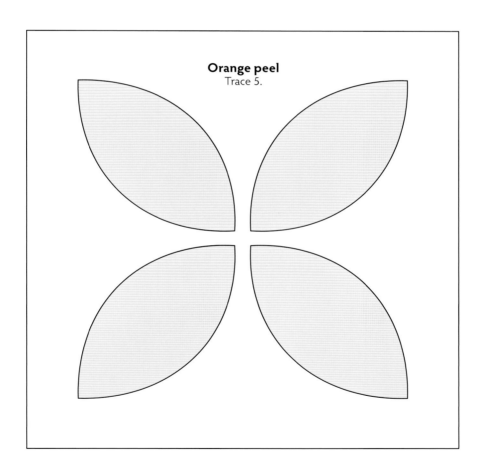

Orange peel
Trace 5.

Appliqué patterns do not
include seam allowances.

Forever Friends

*Some things are just better in pairs. This project yields two coordinating mini-quilts—
one to keep and one to give to a treasured friend. Embellish the corner of the quilt with
a touch of wool appliqué and a sweet embroidered sentiment.*

Finished quilts: 17" × 17" each
Finished block: 3" × 3"

*Designed, pieced, embroidered, and appliquéd
by Lisa Bongean; quilted by Valerie Krueger*

Materials

*The supplies listed are enough to make 2 mini-quilts.
Yardage is based on 42"-wide fabric. Charm squares
are 5"×5".*

1 charm pack of tan, brown, and red prints for blocks
(you'll need 18 tan, 10 brown, and 9 red squares)
1 yard of tan solid for blocks, sashing, border, and
single-fold binding
1 square, 5" × 5", of red wool for appliqué
⅝ yard of fabric for backing
2 squares, 21" × 21", of batting
Primitive Gatherings ¾" half-square-triangle charm
paper*
Removable fabric marker
Fusible web (such as Lite Steam-A-Seam 2)
Coordinating pearl cotton and chenille needle
for appliqué and embroidery

**This piecing paper is designed to efficiently and
accurately make 18 tiny half-square-triangle units
from charm squares.*

Cutting

All measurements include ¼"-wide seam allowances.

From *1* of the brown charm squares, cut:
8 squares, 1¼" × 1¼"

From the tan solid, cut:
3 strips, 3½" × 42"; crosscut into:
- 4 strips, 3½" × 17"
- 4 strips, 3½" × 11"
- 24 rectangles, 1¼" × 3½"
4 strips, 1¼" × 42"

Making the Blocks

Each block is made from one dark (red or brown)
charm square and one tan charm square. Select nine
red and nine brown charm squares. Pair each dark
square with one tan square for a total of 18 pairs. Press
all seam allowances as indicated by the arrows or as
otherwise specified.

1 Place one dark and one tan square right sides
together with the tan square on top. Center one
triangle piecing paper on the tan square. Shorten the
machine stitch length to approximately 1 mm. Sew

along the marked lines on the piecing paper as indicated by the manufacturer's instructions.

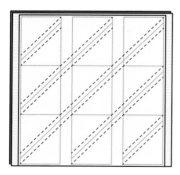

2 Cut through the layers along all of the solid lines as indicated by the manufacturer's instructions. With the paper still in place, press the seam allowances of each half-square triangle. Remove the paper from each unit by bending it away from the fabric and then pulling it from the center close to the seam. Trim away the dog-ears. Each charm square pair will yield 18 half-square-triangle units that are 1¼" square, including seam allowances; 16 are needed for each block.

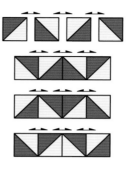

Make 18 units,
1¼" × 1¼", from each pair.

3 Lay out 16 matching half-square-triangle units in four rows of four as shown. Join the units in each row, and then join the rows. The block should measure 3½" square. Make nine brown blocks and nine red blocks.

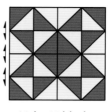

Make 18 blocks,
3½" × 3½".

Assembling the Quilt Tops

1 Lay out the blocks for each quilt top in three rows of three, alternating the brown and red blocks as shown. One quilt top will have five red and four brown blocks, and the other will have four red blocks and five brown blocks.

2 Place a tan 1¼" × 3½" rectangle between the blocks in each row. For the two sashing rows in each quilt, lay out three tan 1¼" × 3½" rectangles

alternating with two brown squares as shown in the quilt assembly diagram. Join the units in each row, and then join the rows. Each quilt center should measure 11" square.

Quilt assembly

3 Sew the tan 3½" × 11" border strips to the sides of each quilt top; press the seam allowances toward the border. Sew the tan 3½" × 17" strips to the top and bottom of each quilt top; press. Each quilt top should measure 17" square.

Embellishing the Quilts

Patterns for the embroidery design and the heart are below. If needed, you can download free instructions about appliqué techniques and embroidery stitches at ShopMartingale.com/HowtoQuilt.

1 Use a removable fabric marker and light box or your preferred transfer method to trace the *forever friends* embroidery design onto each bottom border, referring to the quilt photo on page 144 for placement. Embroider the design using a chenille needle, pearl cotton, and the stem stitch.

2 Trace the heart pattern twice onto the paper side of a piece of fusible web. Fuse the web to the wrong side of the red wool square, and then cut out two hearts along the drawn lines. Remove the paper backing, and then fuse one heart to each quilt, referring to the photo for placement. Hand stitch the edge of each heart using pearl cotton and a blanket stitch or whipstitch.

Finishing the Quilts

For help with the following finishing steps, go to ShopMartingale.com/HowtoQuilt for free, illustrated instructions.

1 Layer and baste the quilt top, batting, and backing. Quilt by hand or machine. The quilts shown are machine quilted in the ditch to outline the shapes of the blocks. The borders are quilted with large curving feathers and parallel lines.

2 Using the tan 1¼"-wide strips, prepare and attach single-fold binding (which some designers prefer to double-fold binding for small quilts).

3 Add a hanging sleeve, if desired.

Heart
Cut 2 from red wool.

Appliqué pattern does not include seam allowance.

Embroidery Key
• French knot
-------- Stem stitch

Parkersburg

Colorful Yankee Puzzle blocks made from alternating light and dark prints create an intricate sea of patchwork surrounding the star of the show, the center appliqué block. If you're new to appliqué, this is a great project for giving it a try.

Finished quilt: 37½" × 37½"
Finished block: 4" × 4"

Designed by Jo Morton; pieced by Sheri Dowding, Mary Fornoff, Cindy Hansen, and Phyllis Masters; quilted by Maggi Honeyman

Swap Talk

A quilt like this may look, or sound, daunting, what with 160 hourglass units needed to make the 40 blocks. But divvy up the task among friends and you can assembly line piece those 2" units and swap them to get a great mix of fabrics and colors for this medallion quilt. Each participant chooses her desired color palette, and then makes blocks for each of the others in the group. Jo's swap consisted of eight quilters, so each person made eight sets of five blocks. Be sure to count yourself in the total number of quilters in the group so that you make a set of blocks for yourself too!

Materials

Yardage is based on 42"-wide fabric. Fat quarters are 18" × 21"; fat eighths are 9" × 21".

⅞ yard *total* of assorted cream shirting prints for Yankee Puzzle blocks

⅞ yard *total* of assorted dark prints in teals, browns, reds, and pinks for Yankee Puzzle blocks

7" × 7" square of light print for center-unit appliqué background

6" × 6" square of teal print for oak-leaf appliqué

5" × 5" square of brown print for small-leaf appliqués

4" × 4" square of medium tan print for center-unit inner-border cornerstones

1 fat eighth of brown stripe for appliqué unit corners

1 fat eighth *each* of brown print and light tan print for center-unit inner border

1 fat quarter of red print for center-unit outer border

1 yard of dark brown print for inner border

1¼ yards of brown floral stripe for outer border

¼ yard of red stripe for single-fold binding

2½ yards of fabric for backing

44" × 44" square of batting

Supplies for your favorite appliqué method

Cutting

All measurements include ¼"-wide seam allowances. You'll need 40 Yankee Puzzle blocks to complete the featured quilt. For ease in piecing the blocks, keep the pieces for each block grouped together as you cut them.

CUTTING FOR 1 BLOCK

From *each* of 2 different cream prints, cut:
1 square, 3¼" × 3¼" (2 total)

From *each* of 2 different dark prints, cut:
1 square, 3¼" × 3¼" (2 total)

ADDITIONAL CUTTING

Cut all pieces across the width of the fabric in the order given unless otherwise noted.

From the brown stripe, cut:
2 squares, 5¾" × 5¾"; cut 1 square in half diagonally from top right to lower left and cut 1 square in half diagonally from top left to lower right to yield a total of 4 triangles

From the light tan print, cut:
4 squares, 3¼" × 3¼"

From the brown print, cut:
16 squares, 1⅞" × 1⅞"

From the medium tan print, cut:
4 squares, 1½" × 1½"

From the *lengthwise* grain of the red print, cut:*
2 strips, 1½" × 10½"
2 strips, 1½" × 12½"

From the *lengthwise* grain of the dark brown print, cut:*
2 strips, 1" × 28½"
2 strips, 1" × 29½"

From the *lengthwise* grain of the brown floral stripe, fussy cut:*
2 strips, 4½" × 29½"
2 strips, 4½" × 37½"

From the red stripe, cut:
4 strips, 1⅛" × 42"

*Jo recommends cutting these pieces on the lengthwise grain (parallel to the selvage) because it has the least amount of stretch and will give you nice, straight edges.

Piecing for One Yankee Puzzle Block

The instructions that follow will make one block. Use the pieces cut for one block and repeat as many times as needed to make the required number of blocks, mixing and matching half-square-triangle units if you're making multiple blocks. Sew all pieces with right sides together using a scant ¼" seam allowance unless otherwise noted. Press all seam allowances as indicated by the arrows or as otherwise specified.

1 Draw a diagonal line from corner to corner on the wrong side of each light 3¼" square.

2 Place a marked light square on top of a dark 3¼" square, right sides together. Sew a scant ¼" from each side of the drawn line. Cut the squares apart on the drawn line to make two half-square-triangle units; press. Repeat for a total of four units. Each unit should measure 2⅞" square, including seam allowances.

Make 4 units,
2⅞" x 2⅞".

3 Draw a diagonal line from corner to corner on the wrong side of two half-square-triangle units made of different prints, marking the line through the sewn seam. Place a marked unit on top of one of the remaining units, positioning the units so the light and dark prints oppose each other. Sew a scant ¼" from each side of the drawn line. Cut apart the units on the drawn line to make two hourglass units. At the seam intersections, cut through both layers of the seam allowance, right up to but not through the stitching. Press the clipped intersections open and press the seam allowances toward the darker prints. Repeat to make a total of four hourglass units measuring 2½" square, including seam allowances.

Make 4 units,
2½" x 2½".

4 Lay out the hourglass units in two horizontal rows of two units each. Join the units in each row; press. Join the rows. Clip the seam intersection. Press the clipped intersection open and press the seam allowances toward the darker print. The block should measure 4½" square, including seam allowances.

Yankee Puzzle block,
4½" x 4½"

Appliquéing and Assembling the Center Unit

The appliqué patterns are provided on page 152. Jo achieves great appliqué results with a technique that combines back-basting and needle-turn, but you can use your own favorite method. You can download complete instructions about a variety of appliqué techniques at ShopMartingale.com/HowtoQuilt.

1 Fold the light 7" square in half diagonally in each direction and lightly finger-press the folds. Using your preferred appliqué technique, cut and prepare:
- 1 oak leaf from the teal 6" square
- 4 small leaves from the brown 5" square

2 Center and stitch the appliqué shapes to the light square using the crease marks for positioning. Square up the appliquéd unit to measure 6¼" square.

3 Sew brown stripe triangles to opposite sides of the appliquéd square, paying close attention to the direction of the stripe. Press. Repeat on the remaining sides of the square; press. Square up the unit to measure 8½" square.

Appliqué block,
8½" x 8½"

4 Draw a diagonal line from corner to corner on the wrong side of the brown print 1⅞" squares. Align two marked squares on opposite corners of a light tan 3¼" square, right sides together. Sew a scant ¼" from both sides of the line. Cut apart on the drawn line to yield two units; press. Place a marked brown square on the corner of the large triangle of each unit, right sides together and with the line oriented as shown. Sew a scant ¼" from both sides of the line. Cut apart on the drawn line to yield two flying-geese units; press. Make a total of 16 flying-geese units. Each unit should measure 1½" × 2½", including seam allowances.

5 Join four flying-geese units side by side to make a center-unit pieced inner-border strip. The strip should measure 1½" × 8½", including seam allowances. Repeat for a total of four pieced inner-border strips.

Make 4 units, 1½" x 8½".

6 Referring to the center-unit assembly diagram at right, pin and then sew pieced inner-border strips to the right and left sides of the appliquéd block, with the tan edges toward the block edges.

7 Join a medium tan 1½" square to each end of the remaining two pieced inner-border strips. Press the seam allowances toward the squares. Pin and then sew these strips to the remaining sides of the center unit, matching seam intersections. Clip the seam intersections at the cornerstones. Press the clipped

intersections open and the seam allowances toward the squares and center. The center unit should now measure 10½" square, including seam allowances.

8 Join the red 1½" × 10½" center-unit border strips to the right and left sides of the center unit. Add the red 1½" × 12½" center-unit border strips to the top and bottom of the center unit. The center unit should measure 12½" square, including seam allowances.

Center-unit assembly

No Fudging on Medallions!

Because the center block is surrounded by a pieced border and then additional patchwork, there's really no room for fudging. So make sure your center unit measures exactly 12½" square before you begin adding the Yankee Puzzle blocks. If your unit is too big or too small, you can adjust the red border as needed by sewing a narrower or deeper seam (same amount on all sides!).

Assembling the Quilt Top

1 Referring to the quilt assembly diagram below, arrange the Yankee Puzzle blocks on your design wall in two horizontal rows of seven blocks each for the top third of the quilt.

2 Sew the first two blocks in each row together. Sew the joined blocks together to make the top-left section. Repeat with the last two blocks in each row to make the top-right section. In the same manner, join the blocks in the middle of each row, and then join the rows to make the top-middle section. Join the sections to complete the top section of the quilt center. Place the section back on the design wall.

3 Repeat steps 1 and 2 to make the bottom section of the quilt center.

4 Place the appliquéd center unit between the top and bottom sections on the design wall. Lay out the remaining Yankee Puzzle blocks in three horizontal rows of two blocks each on each side of the center

unit. Join the blocks in each row. Join the rows on each side of the center unit. Join the block units to the sides of the center unit to complete the center section.

Staying Organized

Pin a note to the top-left section of the quilt center indicating which edge is the top, and then return the section to the design wall. That way, you can be sure when you sew the next section that you have the blocks positioned exactly as you'd laid them out. Step back and look at each section before proceeding, so you can catch any needed changes before you get too far along.

Quilt assembly

5 Join the top and bottom sections to the center section. The pieced quilt top should measure 28½" square, including seam allowances.

6 Sew the dark brown 1" × 28½" strips to the right and left sides of the quilt top. Press the seam allowances toward the border. Join the dark brown 1" × 29½" strips to the top and bottom of the quilt top. Press the seam allowances toward the border. The pieced quilt top should measure 29½" square, including seam allowances.

7 Sew the floral 4½" × 29½" strips to the right and left sides of the quilt top. Press the seam allowances toward the outer border. Add the floral 4½" × 37½" border strips to the top and bottom of the quilt top. Press the seam allowances toward the outer border.

Finishing the Quilt

For help with the following finishing steps, go to ShopMartingale.com/HowtoQuilt for free, illustrated instructions.

1 Layer and baste the quilt top, batting, and backing. Quilt by hand or machine.

2 Using the red stripe 1⅛"-wide strips, prepare and attach single-fold binding (which some designers prefer to double-fold binding for small quilts).

3 Add a hanging sleeve, if desired.

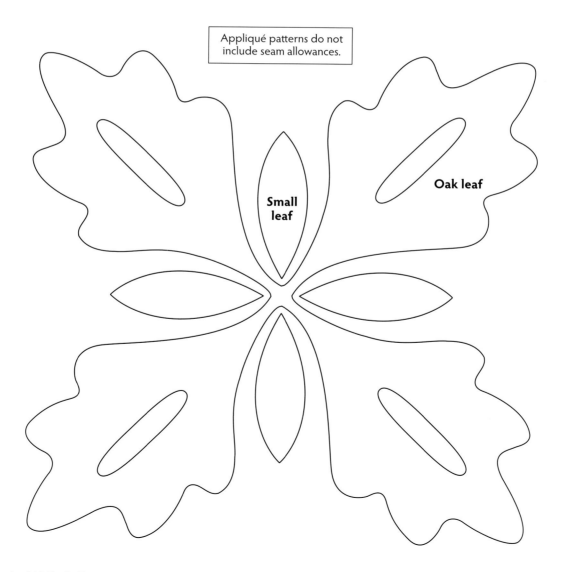

Appliqué patterns do not include seam allowances.

Small leaf

Oak leaf

Strawberry Fields Bird

The little bird in the corner is in for a yummy treat—and so are you, with this delicately embroidered and appliquéd design. To give the Courthouse Steps blocks a cohesive look, consider choosing a pack of 5" precuts in soft, delicate colors.

Finished quilt: 20" × 24½"
Finished block: 4½" × 4½"

Designed and made by Erin Cox

Materials

Yardage is based on 42"-wide fabric.

½ yard *total* of 16 assorted tan or light background prints for blocks and flower appliqués

¼ yard *total* of 4 red prints for blocks and strawberry appliqués

¼ yard *total* of 3 green prints for blocks, strawberry tops, and flower-leaf appliqués

⅛ yard *total* of 4 aqua prints for blocks

⅛ yard *total* of 2 pink prints for blocks

⅛ yard *total* of 2 yellow prints for blocks

⅛ yard of red solid for blocks

⅛ yard of tan print for blocks

⅜ yard of white or cream solid for border

Scrap, at least 3" × 4½", of aqua solid for bird appliqué

⅓ yard of red floral for binding

¾ yard of fabric for backing

¼ yard of 17"-wide paper-backed fusible web

23" × 27" piece of batting

Light-colored thread for appliqué

1 skein of green embroidery floss for vines

1 skein of aqua embroidery floss for bird

1 skein of brown embroidery floss for bird's beak, eye, and legs

Embroidery needle

Removable marking pen

Before You Begin

This quilt is made of 12 blocks, each with a red-solid center square surrounded by logs of four different prints. When the blocks are set together, the print on each side of the block matches the print on the adjacent block, so careful planning up front is essential. To make the layout easier to plan, cutting is organized by light prints and colored prints. You'll be cutting enough pieces from each print to use in two blocks. (Some prints will be used only once; cut this way, you'll have the option of using each color where you'd like.) Once the pieces are cut, use the illustration on page 156 to plan your color placement to ensure your finished Courthouse Steps blocks will form the Chinese lantern effect when sewn together.

Cutting

All measurements include ¼"-wide seam allowances.

From the red solid, cut:
12 squares, 1" × 1"

From *each* of 8 assorted light prints, cut:
2 rectangles, 1" × 2" (16 total)
2 rectangles, 1" × 3" (16 total)
2 rectangles, 1" × 4" (16 total)
2 squares, 1" × 1" (16 total)

Continued on page 154

light rectangles always run vertically. Press all seam allowances toward each newly added piece.

1. Sew two different light print 1" squares to opposite sides of a red-solid square. Then add two different-colored 1" × 2" rectangles to the top and bottom of the center unit as shown.

2. Sewing matching colors together as you go, sew light print 1" × 2" rectangles to the left and right sides of the unit from step 1. Then add colored-print 1" × 3" rectangles to the top and bottom of the center unit as shown.

 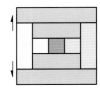

Continued from page 153

From *each* of 8 assorted light prints, cut:
1 rectangle, 1" × 2" (8 total)
1 rectangle, 1" × 3" (8 total)
1 rectangle, 1" × 4" (8 total)
1 square, 1" × 1" (8 total)

From *each* of the green, aqua, pink, yellow, and tan prints, and 3 of the red prints, cut:*
2 rectangles, 1" × 2" (30 total, 6 will be extra)
2 rectangles, 1" × 3" (30 total, 6 will be extra)
2 rectangles, 1" × 4" (30 total, 6 will be extra)
2 rectangles, 1" × 5" (30 total, 6 will be extra)

From the white or cream solid, cut:
2 strips, 3½" × 18½"
2 strips, 3½" × 20"

From the red floral, cut:
3 strips, 2½" × 42"

*The fourth red print will be used for appliqué only.

Making the Blocks

Each block is constructed using two light prints, two colored prints, and one red solid square. The colored rectangles always run horizontally in the blocks. The

3. Continue adding light and colored rectangles, ending with colored-print 1" × 5" rectangles. Make a total of 12 blocks.

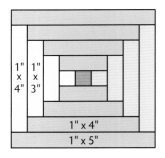

Fabric Placement

Be mindful of the placement of each fabric. You must coordinate the blocks so that the fabrics from top to bottom and side to side match from one block to the next, as shown in the quilt photo above and the assembly diagram on page 156.

Assembling the Quilt Top

Press all seam allowances as indicated by the arrows.

1 Lay out the blocks in four rows of three blocks each as shown in the quilt assembly diagram. Join the blocks into rows. Sew the rows together. The quilt top should measure 14" × 18½".

2 Sew the white or cream 18½"-long strips to the left and right sides of the quilt top. Sew the white or cream 20"-long strips to the top and bottom of the quilt top.

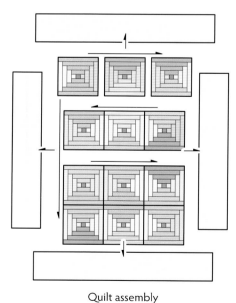

Quilt assembly

Preparing the Appliqués

The patterns for the strawberries, strawberry tops, stem, leaf, flower, flower center, and bird are on page 157. Visit ShopMartingale.com/HowtoQuilt for complete instructions about fusible appliqué and a variety of other techniques.

1 Trace one bird, one of each strawberry and strawberry top, one stem, 18 leaves, eight flowers, and eight flower centers onto the paper side of the fusible web, leaving at least ½" between shapes. Cut out the fusible-web shapes, leaving ⅛" of web outside the traced line.

2 Place the fusible side of each shape on the wrong side of the corresponding fabric. As instructed on the pattern, place the bird on aqua solid; the strawberries on red prints; strawberry tops, stem, and leaves on green prints; flowers on a cream print; and flower centers on a yellow print. Using an iron, fuse the web to the fabric. Cut out the appliqué pieces on the traced lines and remove the paper backing.

3 Referring to the photo on page 154 for placement guidance, draw the embroidered vines onto the borders using a removable marking pen.

4 Position and fuse the appliqué pieces on the border.

Stitching the Appliqués

To prepare your machine for free-motion appliqué, switch to a free-motion foot (also called a darning foot) and lower the feed dogs. Make two or three stitches at the beginning and end of each appliqué step before you lift the presser foot and needle and move to the next appliqué piece.

1 Free-motion stitch around each appliqué piece one time using light-colored thread.

2 Using six strands of embroidery floss and a backstitch, embroider green vines, an aqua bird wing, and a brown beak and legs. Stitch a brown French knot for the bird's eye.

3 Pull all the threads to the back of the border; knot and clip the threads. Press well.

Finishing the Quilt

For help with the following finishing steps, go to ShopMartingale.com/HowtoQuilt for free, illustrated instructions.

1 Layer and baste the quilt top, batting, and backing. Quilt by hand or machine. The quilt shown is stipple quilted using light-colored thread.

2 Using the red floral 2½"-wide strips, prepare and attach double-fold binding.

3 Add a hanging sleeve, if desired.

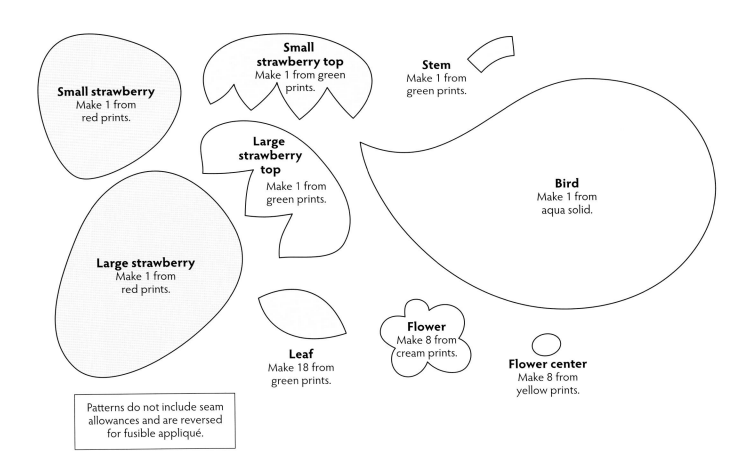

Small strawberry
Make 1 from
red prints.

Small strawberry top
Make 1 from green
prints.

Stem
Make 1 from
green prints.

Large strawberry top
Make 1 from
green prints.

Large strawberry
Make 1 from
red prints.

Bird
Make 1 from
aqua solid.

Leaf
Make 18 from
green prints.

Flower
Make 8 from
cream prints.

Flower center
Make 8 from
yellow prints.

Patterns do not include seam allowances and are reversed for fusible appliqué.

Beach Ball Pinwheels

For a delightfully beachy feel, stitch raw-edged circles to a background of beige squares. Finish the quilt top with an ocean-blue border to make a quilt reminiscent of colorful beach balls scattered across the sparkling sand. (All you need now is the sunscreen!)

Finished quilt: 31½" × 36"
Finished block: 4½" × 4½"

Designed and made by Mary Etherington and Connie Tesene

Materials

Yardage is based on 42"-wide fabric. Charm squares are 5" × 5".

21 charm squares of assorted medium prints for pinwheels
21 charm squares of assorted dark prints for pinwheels
42 charm squares of assorted light prints for backgrounds
⅜ yard of blue print for border
⅓ yard of blue stripe for binding
1¼ yards of fabric for backing
40" × 44" piece of batting
Template plastic

Cutting

All measurements include ¼"-wide seam allowances.

From *each* medium charm square, cut:
2 strips, 2½" × 5"; crosscut into 4 squares, 2½" × 2½".
  Cut in half diagonally to yield 8 triangles (168 total).

From *each* dark charm square, cut:
2 strips, 2½" × 5"; crosscut into 4 squares, 2½" × 2½".
  Cut in half diagonally to yield 8 triangles (168 total).

From the blue print, cut:
4 strips, 2½" × 42"

From the blue stripe, cut:
4 strips, 2¼" × 42"

Making the Blocks

Divide the triangles into 21 groups of eight matching medium triangles and eight matching dark triangles. Each group will make two blocks. Press all seam allowances as indicated by the arrows.

1 Sew a medium triangle to a dark triangle on the diagonal, being careful not to stretch the bias edges. Press the seam allowances toward the dark triangle. The half-square-triangle unit should measure 2⅛" square, including seam allowances. Make eight units using the same medium and dark fabrics.

Make 8.

4 Fold a light charm square in half in both directions and crease to mark the horizontal and vertical centerlines. Place a trimmed pinwheel on the charm square, aligning the seamlines of the pinwheel with the creases on the square. Pin in place and sew the pinwheel to the background, stitching all around the circle ¼" from the raw edge. Make 42 blocks.

Assembling the Quilt Top

1 Arrange the blocks in seven rows of six blocks each. Sew the blocks together into rows, and then join the rows.

2 Sew blue 2½" × 42" strips to the top and bottom edges of the quilt top. Trim the strip ends even with the quilt-top edges.

3 In the same manner, sew the remaining blue 2½" × 42" strips to the sides of the quilt top. Trim the strip ends even with the quilt-top edges.

2 Sew four matching half-square-triangle units together to make a pinwheel unit. The pinwheel should measure 3¾" square, including seam allowances. Make two per matching set for a total of 42.

Make 42.

3 Use the pattern on page 161 to make one circle from template plastic. Center the template on each pinwheel unit and trace. Cut along the traced line.

Make 42.

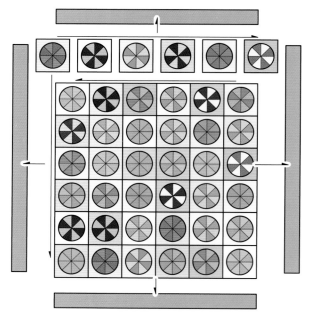

Quilt assembly

Finishing the Quilt

For help with the following finishing steps, go to ShopMartingale.com/HowtoQuilt for free, illustrated instructions.

1 Layer and baste the quilt top, batting, and backing. Quilt by hand or machine. The quilt shown is machine quilted with concentric circles in the pinwheel circles and meander quilting in the block backgrounds. When washed, the edges of the circles will fray.

2 Using the blue stripe 2¼"-wide strips, prepare and attach double-fold binding.

3 Add a hanging sleeve, if desired.

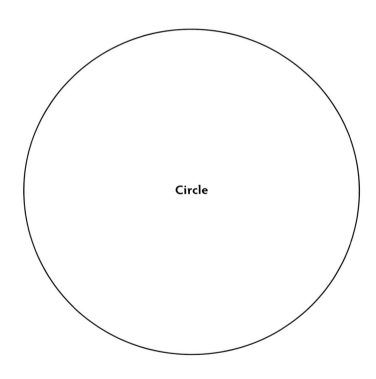

Circle

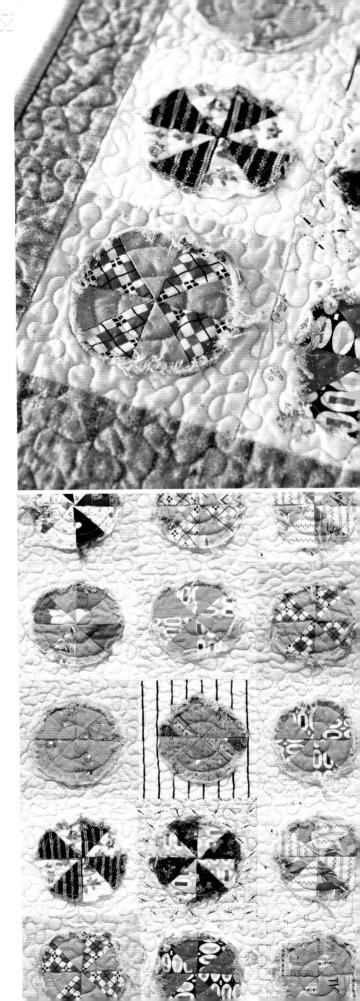

Feels Like Home

A home is many things: a nest, a baseline, a place to rest and reflect. For artistic souls, a home can also be a canvas. Personalize the fabrics in this little banner and give it as a gift, sharing a piece of your heart with someone who has touched your life.

Finished banner:
12½" × 33½"

Designed and made by Pat Sloan

Materials

Yardage is based on 42"-wide fabric.

⅓ yard of cream print for background
½ yard of blue floral for border and single-fold binding
7" × 15" rectangle of green print for stem, flower base, and leaf appliqués
7" × 13" rectangle of red print #1 for petal appliqués
6" × 11" rectangle of red print #2 for house appliqué
4" × 15" rectangle of blue print #1 for letter appliqués
7" × 7" square of blue print #2 for roof appliqué
3" × 8" rectangle of yellow print for door appliqué
3" × 3" square of blue print #3 for chimney appliqué
½ yard of fabric for backing
16" × 40" piece of batting
Supplies for your favorite appliqué method

Cutting

All measurements include ¼"-wide seam allowances.

From the cream print, cut:
1 strip, 7½" × 28½"

From the blue floral, cut:
2 strips, 3" × 28½"
2 strips, 3" × 12½"
3 strips, 1½" × 42"

Assembling the Banner Top

Refer to the assembly diagram to sew the floral 3" × 28½" border strips to the sides of the cream strip. Press the seam allowances toward the border strips. Sew the floral 3" × 12½" border strips to the top and bottom edges of the cream strip. Press the seam allowances toward the border strips.

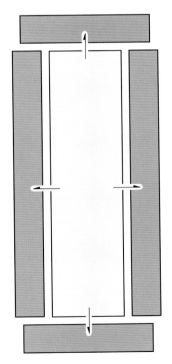

Banner assembly

bottom end under the roof. Arrange three groups of petals on the stem and position a flower base at the bottom of each group. Add the leaves to the stem.

Appliqué placement

Adding the Appliqués

1 Use the patterns on pages 165–167 to prepare the shapes for your favorite method of appliqué from the fabrics indicated.

2 Refer to the appliqué placement diagram above right to position the prepared appliqué shapes on the banner right side in the following order. Place the house, door, roof, and chimney. Position the letters vertically to spell *HOME*. Add the stem, tucking the

3 Fuse the appliqués in place. Blanket-stitch around the outer edges of each shape using a matching or slightly contrasting thread color.

Finishing the Quilt

For help with the following finishing steps, go to ShopMartingale.com/HowtoQuilt for free, illustrated instructions.

1 Layer and baste the quilt top, batting, and backing. Quilt by hand or machine. The quilt shown is outline quilted in all the appliqué shapes. Vertical quilting lines are added to the house, and the roof is quilted with wavy horizontal lines. Open swirls fill the border.

2 Using the blue floral 1½"-wide strips, prepare and attach single-fold binding (which some designers prefer to double-fold binding for small quilts).

3 Add a hanging sleeve, if desired.

Personalize It!

This is a fun little project to make for yourself or as a housewarming or shower gift for a friend. A touch of embroidery is a great way to personalize the banner. Consider stitching the house number or your (or the recipient's) last name.

The Big Book of Little Quilts

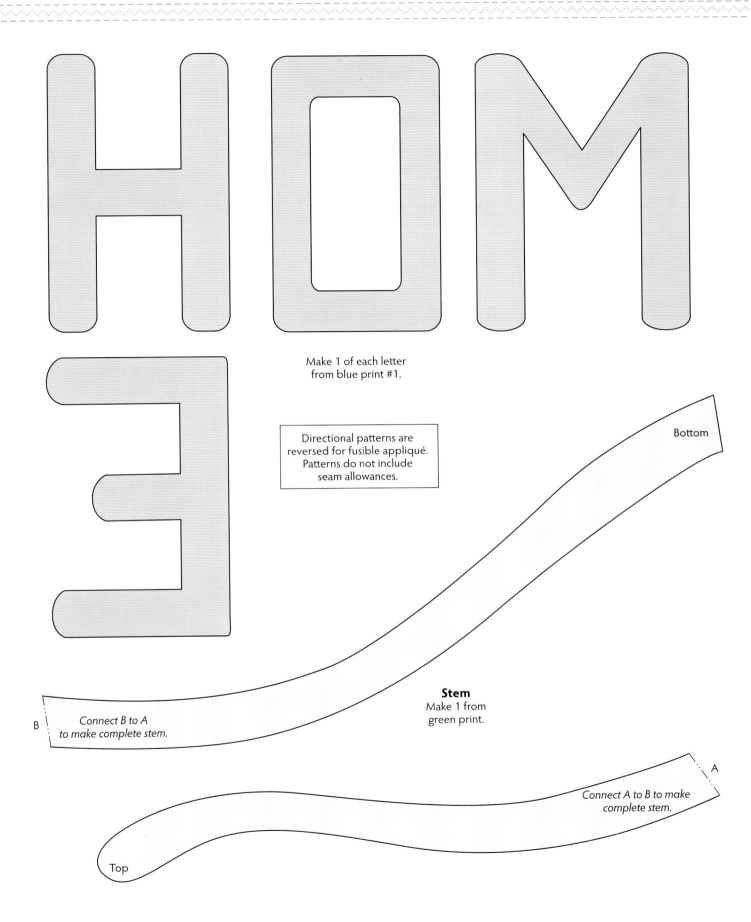

Make 1 of each letter
from blue print #1.

Directional patterns are
reversed for fusible appliqué.
Patterns do not include
seam allowances.

Bottom

Stem
Make 1 from
green print.

B

*Connect B to A
to make complete stem.*

A

*Connect A to B to make
complete stem.*

Top

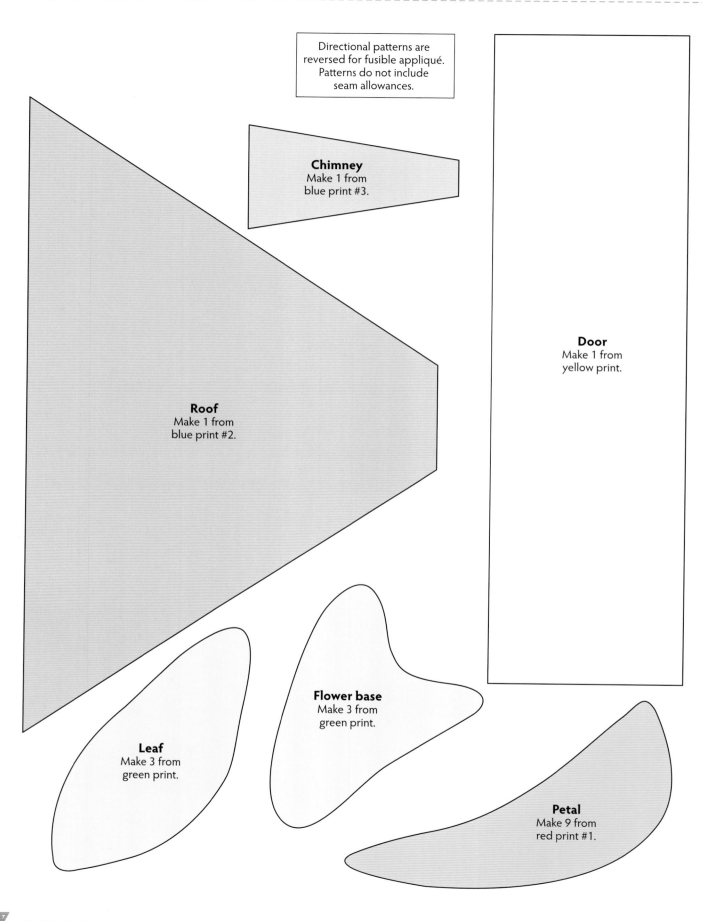

Directional patterns are reversed for fusible appliqué. Patterns do not include seam allowances.

Chimney
Make 1 from blue print #3.

Door
Make 1 from yellow print.

Roof
Make 1 from blue print #2.

Leaf
Make 3 from green print.

Flower base
Make 3 from green print.

Petal
Make 9 from red print #1.

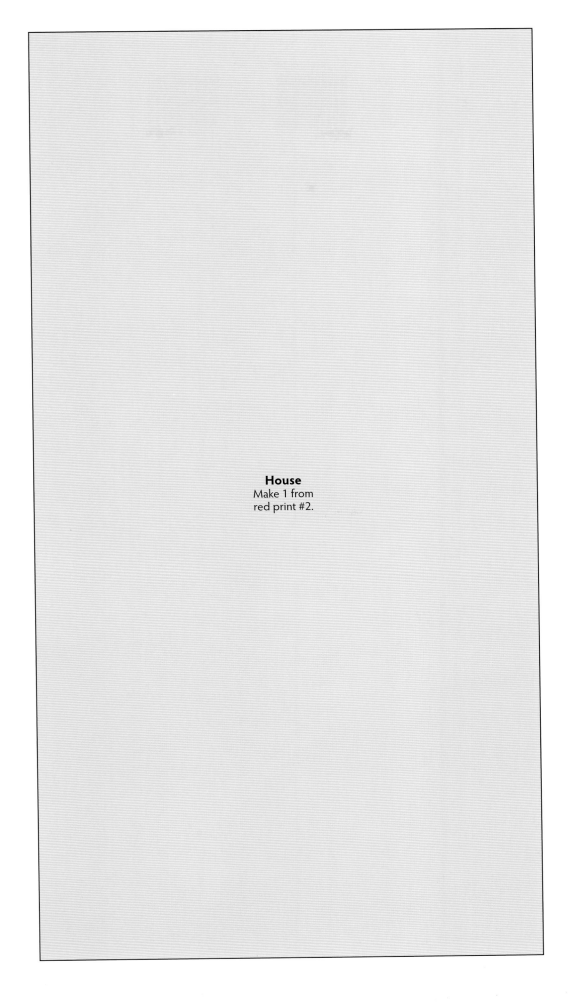

House
Make 1 from
red print #2.

Game Day

*Add a playful touch to your decor with a precut-friendly table topper inspired
by an antique game board. Change the colors to suit your style, hand stitch
the circles in place, and let the fun and games begin!*

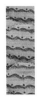

Finished quilt: 28½" × 28½"
Finished block: 8" × 8"

Designed and made by Kathy Schmitz

Materials

Yardage is based on 42"-wide fabric.

77 mini-charm squares, 2½" × 2½", of assorted green,
blue, yellow, and cream prints for blocks, sashing,
and borders

½ yard of cream print for blocks

1 yard of dark blue print for blocks, sashing, borders,
and binding

⅛ yard *each* of 1 yellow, 1 blue, and 2 green prints for
sashing (referred to collectively as "medium prints")

⅛ yard of blue stripe for center block

1 yard of fabric for backing

33" × 33" piece of batting

Cardstock for template

Cutting

All measurements include ¼"-wide seam allowances.

From the cream print, cut:

5 strips, 2½" × 42"; crosscut into:
- 16 rectangles, 2½" × 4½"
- 36 squares, 2½" × 2½"

From the dark blue print, cut:

1 strip, 3" × 42"; crosscut into 13 squares, 3" × 3"

6 strips, 2½" × 42"; crosscut into:
- 12 rectangles, 2½" × 8½"
- 40 squares, 2½" × 2½"

1 strip, 4½" × 42"; crosscut into:
- 5 squares, 4½" × 4½"
- 3 squares, 3" × 3"

4 strips, 2¼" × 42"

From *each* medium print, cut:

4 rectangles, 2½" × 4½" (16 total)

4 squares, 3" × 3" (16 total)

From the blue stripe, cut:

4 rectangles, 2½" × 4½"

Appliquéing the Circles

1 Make a cardstock circle template using the
pattern on page 172. (See "Preparing Appliqué
Circles" on page 170.) Trace the template onto the
wrong side of 77 mini-charm squares. Cut out
the circles, adding a ⅜" seam allowance around
the perimeter.

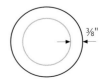

⅜"

3 Hand stitch a cream circle in the center of each dark blue 4½" square. Make five units.

Make 5 units,
4½" × 4½".

4 Hand stitch a circle in the center of 16 cream and eight dark blue 2½" squares.

Make 16 units,   Make 8 units,
2½" × 2½".   2½" × 2½".

5 Place four circles on each dark blue 2½" × 8½" rectangle, spacing them evenly and keeping them ½" from all edges. Hand stitch the circles in place. Make 12 units.

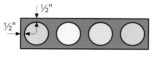

Make 12 units,
2½" × 8½".

Making the Star Blocks

Press the seam allowances as indicated by the arrows.

1 Draw a diagonal line from corner to corner on the wrong side of each remaining cream 2½" square. Place marked squares on opposite corners of an appliquéd dark blue 4½" square as shown. Sew on the drawn lines. Trim the excess corner fabric, ¼" from the stitched line.

2 Using a needle and thread, hand baste around a traced circle, sewing ¼" from the drawn line. Do not clip the thread. Place the cardstock template in the center of the fabric circle. Pull the thread tails to gather the fabric snugly around the template. Knot the thread. Press well. Snip the basting thread and remove the template. Make 77 circles.

Preparing Appliqué Circles

Make 10 to 20 cardstock circle templates so that you can prepare a bunch of circles for appliqué at the same time.

2 In the same manner, sew cream squares to the remaining corners of the dark blue square to make a center unit. Make five units that measure 4½" square, including seam allowances.

Make 5 units,
4½" × 4½".

3 Draw a diagonal line from corner to corner on the wrong side of the remaining dark blue 2½" squares. Place a marked square on one end of a cream 2½" × 4½" rectangle, right sides together. Sew on the drawn line. Trim the excess corner fabric ¼" from the stitched line. Stitch a marked square on the opposite end of the rectangle to make a flying-geese unit. Make 16 units that measure 2½" × 4½", including seam allowances.

Make 16 units,
2½" × 4½".

4 Lay out one center unit, four flying-geese units, and four appliquéd cream squares in three rows. Sew together the pieces in each row. Join the rows to make a Star block. Make four blocks that measure 8½" square, including seam allowances.

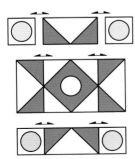 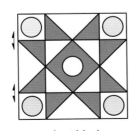

Make 4 blocks,
8½" × 8½".

Making the Center Block

Lay out the remaining center unit, the blue striped rectangles, and four appliquéd dark blue 2½" squares in three rows. Sew together the pieces in each row. Join the rows to make a center block that measures 8½" square, including seam allowances.

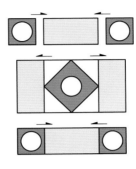 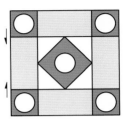

Make 1 block,
8½" × 8½".

Making the Sashing and Borders

1 Draw a diagonal line from corner to corner on the wrong side of each medium print 3" square. Place one marked square on a dark blue 3" square, right sides together. Sew ¼" from both sides of the drawn line. Cut on the line to yield two half-square-triangle units. Trim each unit to measure 2½" square. Make 32 half-square-triangle units.

Make 32 units,
2½" × 2½".

2 Arrange four half-square-triangle units, one of each medium print, as shown. Sew the units together to make a border unit. Make eight units that measure 2½" × 8½", including seam allowances.

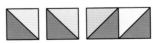 

Make 8 units,
2½" × 8½".

3 Join four medium print rectangles, one of each print, as shown. Make four identical units that measure 4½" × 8½", including seam allowances.

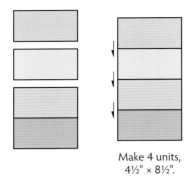

Make 4 units,
4½" × 8½".

4 Sew two appliquéd dark blue rectangles to opposite sides of a unit from step 3 to make a sashing unit. Make four units that measure 8½" square, including seam allowances.

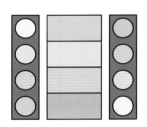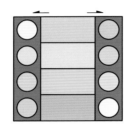

Make 4 units,
8½" × 8½".

Assembling the Quilt Top

1 Arrange the blocks, sashing units, border units, and remaining appliquéd dark blue rectangles and 2½" squares in five rows as shown above right.

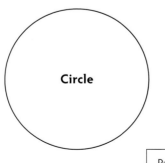

Circle

Pattern does not include
seam allowance.

2 Sew the pieces in each row together. Join the rows to complete the quilt top. The quilt should measure 28½" square.

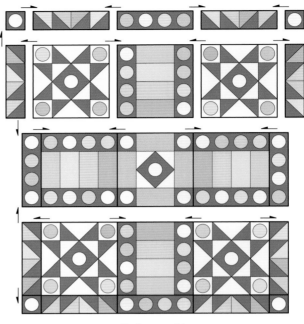

Quilt assembly

Finishing the Quilt

For help with the following finishing steps, go to ShopMartingale.com/HowtoQuilt for free, illustrated instructions.

1 Layer and baste the quilt top, batting, and backing. Quilt by hand or machine. The quilt shown is machine quilted around the appliquéd circles, with curved outlines in the half-square-triangle units and rows of circles in the sashing rectangles.

2 Using the dark blue 2¼"-wide strips, prepare and attach double-fold binding.

3 Add a hanging sleeve, if desired.

Star Flowers and Berries

A plaid background filled with meander-stitch quilting adds visual texture to an appliquéd topiary. The Sawtooth outer border echoes the repetition of squares. Design tip from Jo: hang a quilt in front of a small ho-hum window, and instantly improve your view!

Finished quilt:
20½" × 28½"

Designed and made by Jo Morton

Materials

Yardage is based on 42"-wide fabric.

⅔ yard of tan plaid for appliqué background

8" × 8" square of dark red plaid for vase appliqué

⅓ yard *total* of assorted green prints for stem and leaf appliqués

¼ yard *total* of assorted yellow prints for circle appliqués

3 squares, 5" × 5", of assorted dark red prints for star flower appliqués

⅔ yard of green print for inner border

⅝ yard of dark red print for Sawtooth outer border and single-fold binding

⅜ yard of caramel vine print for Sawtooth outer border

⅔ yard of fabric for backing

25" × 33" piece of batting

Template plastic, freezer paper, or fusible web for preparing shapes for your favorite appliqué method

Cutting

All measurements include ¼"-wide seam allowances.

From the *lengthwise* grain of the tan plaid, cut:*
1 rectangle, 15" × 23"

From the *lengthwise* grain of the green print, cut:*
2 strips, 1½" × 22½"
2 strips, 1½" × 16½"

From the *crosswise* grain of the dark red print, cut:
3 strips, 1⅛" × 42"

From the remaining dark red print, cut:
6 squares, 6" × 6"

From the caramel vine print, cut:
6 squares, 6" × 6"

*Jo recommends cutting these pieces on the lengthwise grain (parallel to the selvage) because it has the least amount of stretch and will give you nice, straight edges.

Appliquéing the Quilt Center

Use your favorite appliqué method. Visit ShopMartingale.com/HowtoQuilt for complete instructions about a variety of techniques.

1 Prepare the following appliqués using patterns A–H on page 176 and referring to the materials list and quilt photo for fabric colors:

- 1 of A (vase)
- 1 of B (stem)
- 1 each of C and C reversed (stems)
- 1 each of D and D reversed (stems)
- 2 each of E and E reversed (leaves)
- 1 each of F and F reversed (leaves)
- 3 of G (star flowers)
- 19 of H (circles)

Adding the Inner Border

Press all seam allowances as indicated by the arrows.

Sew the green 1½" × 22½" strips to the sides of the appliquéd background rectangle. Sew the green 1½" × 16½" strips to the top and bottom of the background rectangle.

2 Place the appliqué shapes on the tan-plaid 15" × 23" background. Pin or baste the pieces in place.

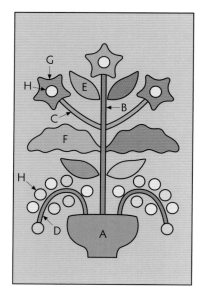

Appliqué placement diagram

3 Appliqué the shapes by hand or machine.

4 Trim the background to measure 14½" × 22½".

Making the Sawtooth Outer Border

You will need a total of 44 half-square-triangle units for the outer border.

1 Draw two diagonal lines from corner to corner on the wrong side of each caramel vine-print 6" square.

2 Lay a marked caramel vine-print square on top of a dark red 6" square right sides together. Sew a scant ¼" from each side of the drawn lines.

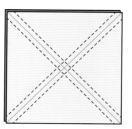

3 Cut the sewn squares apart *first* horizontally and then vertically to make four segments.

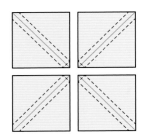

4 Cut each segment apart on the drawn diagonal line to make eight half-square-triangle units (each segment yields two half-square-triangle units). Trim each unit to measure 2½" × 2½".

5 Repeat steps 2–4 to make a total of 48 half-square-triangle units. (You will use 44.)

6 Lay out 12 half-square-triangle units in a row, with the dark red triangle toward the outer edge. Sew the units together to make a side border strip. The side border strip should measure 2½" × 24½". Repeat to make a second side border strip.

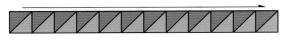

Side outer border.
Make 2.

7 Lay out 10 half-square-triangle units in a row, with the dark red triangle toward the outer edge except for one unit on the left end of the row. Sew the units together to make a top border strip. The top border strip should measure 2½" × 20½". Repeat to make a bottom border strip.

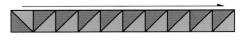

Top/bottom outer border.
Make 2.

8 Pin and sew the side border strips to the quilt top, making sure the light triangles are adjoining the inner border. Pin and sew the top and bottom border strips to the remaining sides, again with the light triangles adjoining the inner border.

Quilt assembly

Finishing the Quilt

For help with the following finishing steps, go to ShopMartingale.com/HowtoQuilt for free, illustrated instructions.

1 Layer and baste the quilt top, batting, and backing. Quilt by hand or machine. The quilt shown is machine quilted around each appliqué. Vein accents are added to the leaves, a star is added in each flower, and horizontal lines are quilted in the vase. A meandering stitch is used to fill the plaid background. Parallel lines are quilted along the inner border and in the ditch of the outer border, with zigzag lines echoing the sawtooth angles.

2 Using the dark red 1⅛"-wide strips, prepare and attach single-fold binding (which some designers prefer to double-fold binding for small quilts).

3 Add a hanging sleeve, if desired.

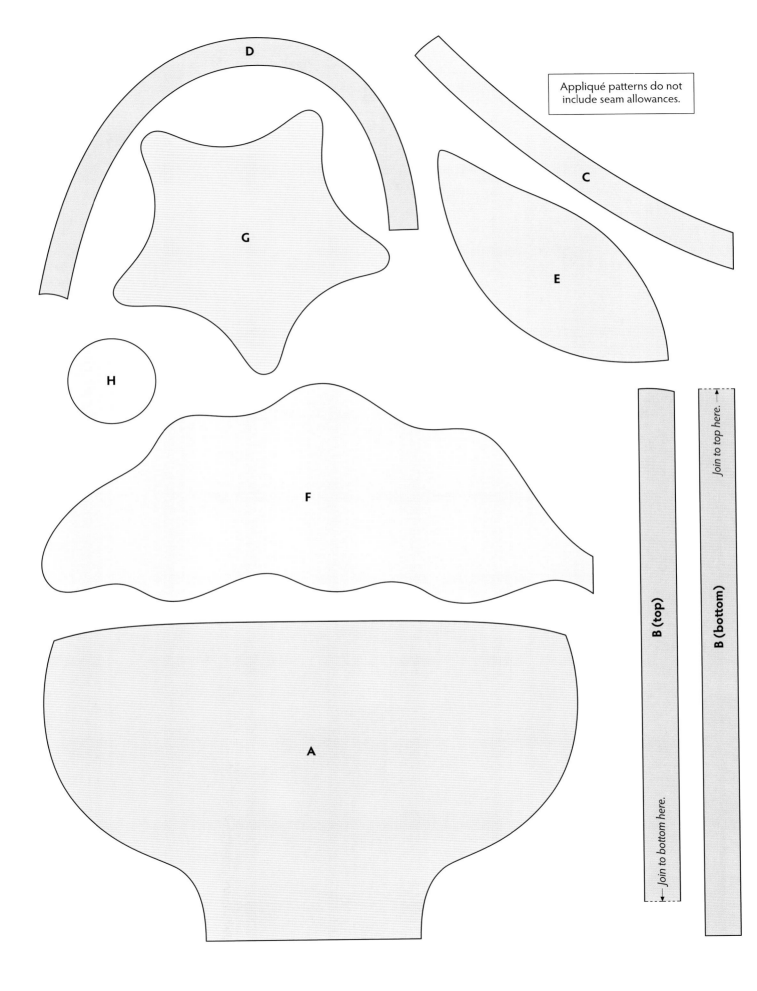

D

Appliqué patterns do not
include seam allowances.

C

G

E

H

F

B (top)

Join to top here.

B (bottom)

Join to bottom here.

A

Bird Family

Birds of a feather flock adorably together on a stitched tree branch. You can tweak the design to represent your own brood or a friend's family; simply appliqué one bird for each family member. Aqua and yellow give this cheerful little quilt a modern vibe.

Finished quilt:
17" × 11"

Designed and made by Erin Cox

Materials

Yardage is based on 42"-wide fabric. Fat quarters are 18" × 21".

¼ yard of natural-colored linen for appliqué background

¼ yard *total* of assorted yellow prints for patchwork border and bird appliqués

¼ yard *total* of assorted aqua prints for patchwork border and bird appliqués

¼ yard of aqua dot for binding

1 fat quarter of fabric for backing

14" × 20" piece of batting

6" × 15" piece of lightweight fusible interfacing

4" × 8" piece of lightweight fusible web

Black thread for appliqué

Cutting

All measurements include ¼"-wide seam allowances.

From the natural-colored linen, cut:
1 rectangle, 6" × 15"

From the assorted yellow prints, cut:
25 squares, 2" × 2"

From the assorted aqua prints, cut:
25 squares, 2" × 2"

From the aqua dot, cut:
2 strips, 2½" × 42"

Preparing the Appliqués

The patterns for the birds are on page 181. Visit ShopMartingale.com/HowtoQuilt for complete instructions about fusible appliqué and a variety of other techniques.

1 Place the interfacing fusible side down on the linen rectangle. Press until fused. Set aside.

2 Trace the number of birds indicated on the patterns onto the paper side of the fusible web, leaving at least ½" between shapes. Cut out the fusible-web shapes, leaving ⅛" of web outside the traced line.

3 Place the fusible side of each shape onto the wrong side of the corresponding fabric. As instructed on the patterns, place two birds on aqua prints and three birds on yellow prints. Using an iron, fuse the web to the fabric.

4 Cut out the appliqué pieces on the traced lines and remove the paper backing.

5 Find the center of the linen rectangle by gently pressing the piece in half vertically and horizontally.

3 Lift the presser foot and needle and move to the area of the bird where the eye should be; sew in a circular motion to make a small eye for the bird.

4 Move to the bottom or belly of the bird and stitch two parallel lines about ⅛" to ¼" apart to make the bird's legs.

5 Repeat steps 1–4 to stitch around each bird.

6 About 1½" from the left edge of the linen, start stitching the branch that the birds rest on. Stitch toward the right, stopping about 1½" from the edge of the linen. Go back to the left side and then back to the right side again, making sure that your stitching lines touch the birds' legs.

Start stitching.

7 Pull all the threads to the back of the linen background; knot and clip the threads.

8 Press well. Trim the appliquéd piece to measure 14" × 5", trimming equally on all sides.

6 Center the bird appliqués on the linen, spacing them about ½" to ¾" apart and leaving at least 1½" in from each side of the linen. Fuse in place.

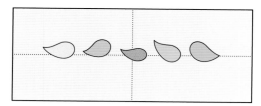

Appliqué placement guide

Stitching the Appliqués

To prepare your machine for free-motion appliqué, switch to a free-motion foot (also called a darning foot) and lower the feed dogs. Make two or three stitches at the beginning and end of each appliqué step before you lift the presser foot and needle and move to the next appliqué piece.

1 Starting along the round side of a bird, sew along the edge of the appliqué piece until you have gone around the bird completely one time. Sew around the bird one more time.

Start stitching.

2 Stitch a triangular-shaped beak onto the linen at the spot where you began. Sew over this one more time.

Adding the Patchwork Border

Replace the free-motion foot with your general sewing presser foot. Press all seam allowances as indicated by the arrows.

1 Arrange the aqua and yellow squares in a pleasing manner around the appliquéd piece as shown in the photo above left.

2 Sew three squares together to make a side border. Repeat to make a second side border.

Make 2.

3 Sew 11 squares together to make a strip. Repeat to make a second strip, and then sew the strips together to make the top border. Repeat to make the bottom border.

Make 2.

4 Sew the borders from step 2 to the left and right sides of the appliquéd piece. Sew the borders from step 3 to the top and bottom.

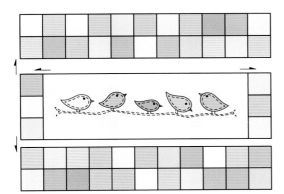

Finishing the Quilt

For help with the following finishing steps, go to ShopMartingale.com/HowtoQuilt for free, illustrated instructions.

1 Layer and baste the quilt top, batting, and backing. Quilt by hand or machine. The quilt shown is outline quilted ⅛" from the edge of the patchwork. Then two parallel lines are stitched, starting ½" from the first line and spaced ½" apart.

2 Using the aqua dot 2½"-wide strips, prepare and attach double-fold binding.

3 Add a hanging sleeve, if desired.

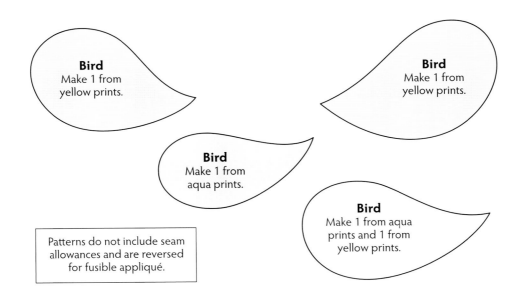

Bird
Make 1 from yellow prints.

Bird
Make 1 from yellow prints.

Bird
Make 1 from aqua prints.

Bird
Make 1 from aqua prints and 1 from yellow prints.

Patterns do not include seam allowances and are reversed for fusible appliqué.

Oak Patch

With its undeniable charm and versatility, the classic Nine Patch block has been favored by generations of quiltmakers. Endless setting and size options allow this block to be used in the humblest of quilts, or it can be "dressed to the nines" to steal the spotlight.

Finished quilt: 39½" × 39½"
Finished block: 3" × 3"

Designed by Kim Diehl; pieced by Connie Tabor and Kim Diehl; machine appliquéd by Kim Diehl; machine quilted by Karen Brown

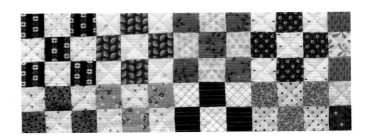

Materials

Yardage is based on 42"-wide fabric. Fat quarters are 18" × 21"; chubby sixteenths are 9" × 10½".

44 squares, 5" × 5" *each*, of assorted dark prints in autumn colors for Nine Patch blocks

44 squares, 5" × 5" *each*, of assorted light prints for Nine Patch blocks

⅞ yard of coordinating light print for appliqué blocks and sashing

½ yard of black print for mini nine-patch units and binding

¼ yard (not a fat quarter) of light brown print for sashing

1 fat quarter of medium brown print for swag appliqués

2 chubby sixteenths of different red prints for oak-leaf appliqués

1 chubby sixteenth of orange print for oak-leaf appliqués

1 chubby sixteenth of gold print for oak-leaf appliqués

3 chubby sixteenths of assorted green prints for small-leaf appliqués

2⅝ yards of fabric for backing

46" × 46" square of batting

Supplies for your favorite traditional appliqué method

Cutting

All measurements include ¼"-wide seam allowances. You'll need 44 of each style of Nine Patch block (88 total). For ease in piecing the blocks, keep the pieces for each block together as you cut them.

CUTTING FOR 1 DARK-CORNER AND 1 LIGHT-CORNER NINE PATCH BLOCK

From 1 dark print 5" square, cut:
9 squares, 1½" × 1½"

From 1 light print 5" square, cut:
9 squares, 1½" × 1½"

ADDITIONAL CUTTING

Cut pieces across the width of the fabric in the order given. Cutting instructions for appliqués are provided separately.

From the coordinating light print, cut:
2 strips, 1½" × 42"
2 strips, 1" × 42"; crosscut *1 strip* in half to make 2 strips, 1" × 21"
4 strips, 4¼" × 42"; crosscut into:
   • 8 rectangles, 4¼" × 12½"
   • 8 rectangles, 4¼" × 5"
1 strip, 2" × 42"; crosscut into 16 squares, 2" × 2"
5 squares, 1½" × 1½"

Continued on page 184

squares in three horizontal rows. Join the pieces in each row. Join the rows. The block should measure 3½" square, including seam allowances.

Make 1 block,
3½" x 3½".

2 To make the light-corner Nine Patch block, lay out four dark 1½" squares and five light 1½" squares in three horizontal rows. Join the pieces in each row. Join the rows. The pieced block should measure 3½" square, including seam allowances.

Make 1 block,
3½" x 3½".

3 Repeat steps 1 and 2 to make 88 Nine Patch blocks (44 of each).

Piecing the Mini Nine-Patch Units

1 Using the 1" × 42" strips, join a black strip to each long edge of a coordinating light strip to make strip set A; press. Crosscut the strip set into 40 segments, 1" wide.

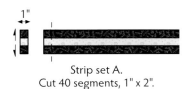

Strip set A.
Cut 40 segments, 1" x 2".

Continued from page 183

From the black print, cut:
5 strips, 2½" × 42"
2 strips, 1" × 42"
1 strip, 1" × 21"

From the light brown print, cut:
5 strips, 1½" × 42"; crosscut *1 strip* into 4 squares, 1½" × 1½"

Piecing for Two Nine Patch Blocks

The instructions that follow will make one Nine Patch block with dark corners and one with light corners. Use the pieces cut for one pair of blocks and repeat as often as needed to make the required number of blocks. Sew all pieces with right sides together using a ¼" seam allowance unless otherwise noted. Press all seam allowances as indicated by the arrows or as otherwise specified.

1 To make the dark-corner Nine Patch block, lay out five dark 1½" squares and four light 1½"

2 Using the 1" × 21" strips, join a coordinating light strip to each long edge of a black strip to make strip set B. Crosscut the strip set into 20 segments, 1" wide.

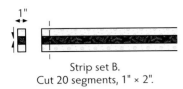

Strip set B.
Cut 20 segments, 1" × 2".

3 Sew an A segment to each long edge of a B segment. Repeat to make a total of 20 mini nine-patch units measuring 2" square, including seam allowances.

Make 20 units,
2" x 2".

Assembling the Appliqué Backgrounds

1 Lay out five mini nine-patch units and four coordinating light 2" squares in three horizontal rows. Join the pieces in each row. Join the rows. Repeat to make a total of four double nine-patch units measuring 5" square, including seam allowances.

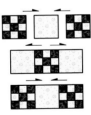

Make 4 units, 5" x 5".

Correcting Inaccurate Patchwork

Sometimes your blocks aren't accurate in size . . . it just happens! Before tossing these onto the scrap heap, follow Kim Diehl's suggestions for turning lemons into lemonade and attempting corrections. For blocks that are too large, try giving them a generous misting of Best Press (or, as an alternative, set your iron to the steam setting), and then press the block to help shrink the fabric. Once the block has cooled, use your rotary cutter and acrylic ruler to square it up and trim away any excess seam allowance.

For blocks that are too small, set your iron to a hot, dry setting. Position a block right side up on your pressing board and brace one side edge with your hand. Beginning at the center of the block, gently but firmly smooth the iron toward the outer edge. Rotate and repeat with each remaining side of the block. This little trick can help relax and stretch the fibers of the cloth slightly, thus potentially allowing you to salvage a block that would otherwise be unusable.

2 Join light 4¼" × 5" rectangles to the right and left sides of a double nine-patch unit; press. Join light 4¼" × 12½" rectangles to the remaining sides of the unit. Repeat to make a total of four appliqué block backgrounds measuring 12½" square, including seam allowances.

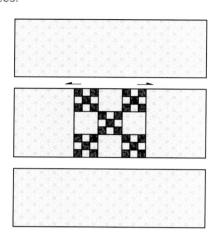

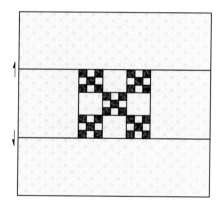

Make 4 blocks, 12½" x 12½".

Appliquéing the Blocks

The appliqué patterns are provided on page 188. Visit ShopMartingale.com/HowtoQuilt for complete instructions about a variety of techniques.

1 Using your preferred method, cut and prepare the following appliqués:
- 16 swags from medium brown print
- 4 oak leaves from each of the two red chubby sixteenths, the orange chubby sixteenth, and the gold chubby sixteenth (16 total)
- 32 small leaves total from the three assorted green chubby sixteenths

2 With right sides together, fold an appliqué block foundation in half lengthwise; use a hot, dry iron to lightly press a center crease. Open the block, and then continue folding and pressing to add a horizontal crease and two diagonal creases.

3 Referring to the pictured quilt, fold four swags in half to find the centers, and lightly finger-press the creases. Position a swag onto each side of the center double nine-patch unit, with the tips resting against the seams of the unit; pin or baste. Appliqué the swags in place.

4 Referring to the photo on page 184 for color placement (or positioning the colors randomly if you wish), lay out two red oak leaves, one orange oak leaf, and one gold oak leaf, with the inner points resting between the swags and the tips centered over the diagonal block creases; pin or baste. Appliqué the leaves in place.

5 Position, baste, and appliqué two small leaves along the curved outer edge of each swag.

6 Repeat steps 2–5 to complete four appliqué blocks measuring 12½" square, including seam allowances.

Assembling the Quilt Top

1 Join light brown 1½" × 42" strips to both long sides of a coordinating light 1½" × 42" strip to make a pieced strip set C; press. Repeat for a total of two strip sets. Crosscut the strip sets into four segments, 12½" wide, for the pieced sashing strips.

Strip set C. Make 2.
Cut 4 segments, 3½" x 12½".

2 Referring to "Piecing for Two Nine Patch Blocks" (page 184), use the five coordinating light 1½" squares and the four light brown 1½" squares to make a nine-patch unit with light corners measuring 3½" square, including seam allowances.

3 Lay out the appliquéd blocks, the pieced sashing strips, and the nine-patch unit in three horizontal rows. Join the pieces in each row. Join the rows. The quilt center should measure 27½" square, including seam allowances.

Adding the Nine Patch Border

1 Lay out five light-corner Nine Patch blocks and four dark-corner Nine Patch blocks in alternating positions. Join the blocks. Repeat to make a total of two short A border strips measuring 3½" × 27½", including seam allowances.

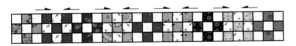

Border A.
Make 2.

2 Repeat step 1 using five dark-corner Nine Patch blocks and four light-corner Nine Patch blocks, reversing the block placement, to make two short B border strips.

Border B.
Make 2.

3 Join a short A border strip to a short B border strip. Repeat to make two short border strips measuring 6½" × 27½", including seam allowances. Using the pictured quilt as a guide, join the strip A edges to the right and left sides of the quilt center. Press the seam allowances toward the border.

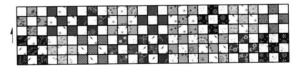

Side borders.
Make 2.

4 Repeat step 1 using seven light-corner Nine Patch blocks and six dark-corner Nine Patch blocks to make two long A border strips measuring 3½" × 39½", including seam allowances. In the same manner, use seven dark-corner Nine Patch blocks and six light-corner Nine Patch blocks, reversing the block placement, to make two long B border strips.

5 Join a long A border strip to a long B border strip. Press the seam allowances toward border B. Repeat to make two pieced long border strips measuring 6½" × 39½", including seam allowances. Using the pictured quilt as a guide, join the strip A edges to the remaining sides of the quilt center. Press the seam allowances toward the border.

Finishing the Quilt

For help with the following finishing steps, go to ShopMartingale.com/HowtoQuilt for free, illustrated instructions.

1 Layer and baste the quilt top, batting, and backing. Quilt by hand or machine. The blocks of the featured quilt are machine quilted with small feathered wreaths around the center portion of the double nine-patch units, the appliqués are outlined to emphasize their shapes, and a small-scale stipple design is used to fill the open background areas. Xs are stitched onto the border Nine Patch blocks, with feathered vines radiating out from the center-most Nine Patch along the center sashing strips.

2 Using the black 2½"-wide strips, prepare and attach double-fold binding.

3 Add a hanging sleeve, if desired.

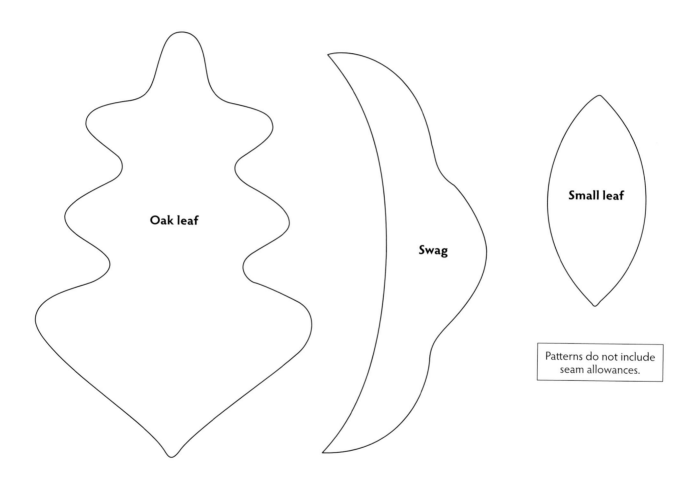

Oak leaf

Swag

Small leaf

Patterns do not include seam allowances.

Bedford Reels

This quilt provides a beautiful setting for petite appliquéd Reel blocks. Think of stitching these blocks as your take-along project—you'll have them done sooner than you think. Choose a palette of richly colored prints inspired by treasured heirlooms or artwork.

Finished quilt: 36⅛" × 36⅛"
Finished block: 4" × 4"

*Designed, pieced, and appliquéd by Jo Morton;
quilted by Lori Kukuk*

Materials

Yardage is based on 42"-wide fabric. Fat quarters are 18" × 21".

1 yard *total* of assorted light prints for blocks and border 2
1⅛ yards *total* of assorted medium to dark prints for blocks and border 2
1 fat quarter of green print for setting triangles
⅞ yard of red print for border 1
1 yard of pink print for border 3
1⅛ yards of red floral for border 4
¼ yard of red stripe for single-fold binding
1⅛ yards of fabric for backing
40" × 40" piece of batting
Supplies for your favorite appliqué method

Cutting

All measurements include ¼"-wide seam allowances. Cut the border strips on the lengthwise grain (parallel to the selvage) because it has the least amount of stretch.

From the assorted light prints, cut:
16 squares, 5" × 5"
9 squares, 3½" × 3½", for reel appliqués
9 squares, 4" × 4", for jack appliqués
38 squares, 2¼" × 2¼"
2 squares, 1¾" × 1¾"

From the assorted medium to dark prints, cut:
9 squares, 5" × 5"
16 squares, 3½" × 3½", for reel appliqués
16 squares, 4" × 4", for jack appliqués
38 squares, 2¼" × 2¼"
2 squares, 1¾" × 1¾"

From the green print, cut:
3 squares, 7½" × 7½"; cut into quarters diagonally to yield 12 triangles
2 squares, 4¼" × 4¼"; cut in half diagonally to yield 4 triangles

From the *lengthwise* grain of the red print, cut:
2 strips, 1¼" × 23⅛"
2 strips, 1¼" × 24⅝"

From the *lengthwise* grain of the pink print, cut:*
2 strips, 1¼" × 27⅛"
2 strips, 1¼" × 28⅝"

From the *lengthwise* grain of the red floral, cut:
2 strips, 4¼" × 28⅝"
2 strips, 4¼" × 36⅛"

From the red stripe, cut:
4 strips, 1⅛" × 42"

*Jo fussy cut these border strips, but you may not want or need to, depending on your fabric.

Appliquéing the Blocks

Patterns are on page 193. Jo appliquéd the blocks using her favorite method, back-basting appliqué. If you use this technique, you do not need to create templates or cut the appliqué shapes beforehand. You can, of course, use your own preferred method of appliqué. Visit ShopMartingale.com/HowtoQuilt for complete instructions about a variety of techniques.

1 Using the pattern for the reel and a medium or dark 3½" square, appliqué the shape to a light print 5" background square. Using the pattern for the jack and a medium or dark 4" square, appliqué the shape to the background. Jo used two fabrics for some of the appliqués and just one fabric for others.

2 After the stitching is complete, trim the appliqué block to 4½" × 4½", including seam allowances. Make 16 blocks with light backgrounds and 9 blocks with medium or dark backgrounds.

Make 16 blocks;
trim to 4½" × 4½".

Make 9 blocks;
trim to 4½" × 4½".

Assembling the Quilt Top

Press all seam allowances as indicated by the arrows.

1 Referring to the assembly diagram below, arrange the blocks with light backgrounds on point in four rows of four blocks each. Fill in the nine openings with the blocks that have dark backgrounds. Add the green print 7½" side triangles along all four edges. Sew into diagonal rows. Pin, matching seam intersections, and then sew the rows together. At the seam intersections, cut through both layers of the seam allowance, right up to but not through the stitching. Press the seam allowances toward the dark background blocks and toward the setting triangles. Press the clipped intersections open. Sew a green print 4¼" half-square triangle to each corner of the top, and press.

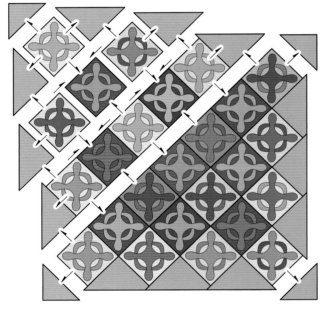

Quilt assembly

2 Trim the quilt center to measure 23⅛" square, including seam allowances.

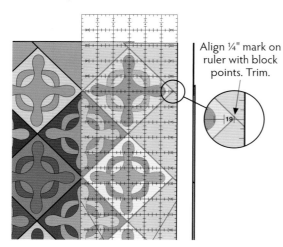

Align ¼" mark on ruler with block points. Trim.

Trim center to 23⅛" × 23⅛".

Adding the Borders

1 Sew the red print 1¼" × 23⅛" strips to opposite sides of the quilt top. Sew the red print 1¼" × 24⅝" strips to the top and bottom of the quilt top. The quilt top should measure 24⅝" square, including seam allowances.

2 Pair a dark and a light 2¼" square. Draw a diagonal line from corner to corner on the wrong side of the light square. Align the squares with right sides together and sew a scant ¼" from each side of the drawn line. Cut on the drawn line and carefully press. Repeat with all of the 2¼" squares to make 76 half-square-triangle units. Trim each unit to measure 1¾" square.

  1¾"
1¾"

Make 76 units.

3 Arrange the half-square-triangle units around the quilt center with the light triangles toward the center. There should be 19 units per side. Add the four 1¾" corner squares, with the dark and the light in opposite corners; the dark squares should be next to light triangles and the light squares should be next to dark triangles.

4 Sew each group of 19 half-square-triangle units together in a row to make four border strips (see "Fitting Finesse" below). Carefully press the seam allowances open to distribute the bulk. The border strips should measure 24⅝" in length. Add the 1¾" squares to the ends of two of the strips and press.

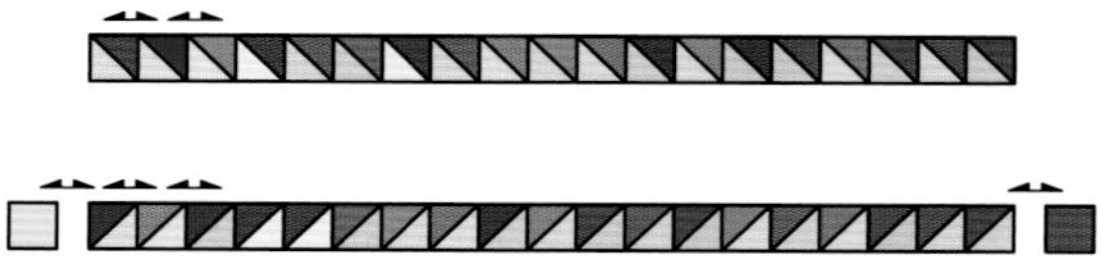

Make 2 of each border.

5 Pin and sew the short borders to opposite sides of the quilt top, with light sides toward the center. Press. Pin and sew the long borders to the top and bottom of the quilt top, with light sides toward the center. Clip the seam allowances at the corner seam intersections and press. Continue to press toward the border and press the clipped intersections open. The quilt top should measure 27⅛" square, including seam allowances.

Fitting Finesse

Jo cautions that the math isn't exact for the half-square-triangle border, as 19 × 1¼" = 24¼", including seam allowances. The quilt center should measure 24⅝", so she advises taking a few scant seam allowances as necessary when sewing each group of 19 half-square-triangle units together, and it should work just fine.

6 Sew the two pink print 1¼" × 27⅛" strips to opposite sides of the quilt and press. Sew the two pink print 1¼" × 28⅝" strips to the top and bottom of the quilt and press. The top should now measure 28⅝" square, including seam allowances.

7 Sew the two red floral 4¼" × 28⅝" strips to the sides of the quilt top and press. Sew the red floral 4¼" × 36⅛" strips to the top and bottom of the quilt top and press. The quilt top should measure 36⅛" square.

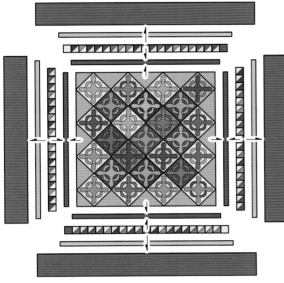

Adding borders

Finishing the Quilt

For help with the following finishing steps, go to ShopMartingale.com/HowtoQuilt for free, illustrated instructions.

1 Layer and baste the quilt top, batting, and backing. Quilt by hand or machine. The quilt shown is machine quilted in the ditch around each reel, with a line of echo quilting about ¼" away. The green setting triangles are quilted in a chevron pattern. The inner red border, triangle border, and pink border are quilted in the ditch on both sides, and a beautiful feather motif is added to the red floral border. Thread colors are changed throughout the quilting to coordinate with the fabrics.

2 Using the red stripe 1⅛"-wide strips, prepare and attach single-fold binding (which some designers prefer to double-fold binding for small quilts).

3 Add a hanging sleeve, if desired.

Appliqué patterns do not include seam allowances.

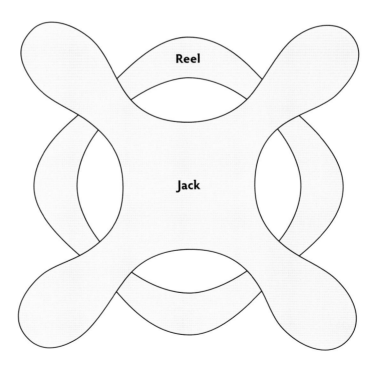

Dresden Candy Dish

Dresden plates create a classic quilt block, but if you think there's nothing new you can do with them, think again. Pat got creative by sewing 2½" squares into pairs and then cutting Dresden blades from the units.

Finished quilt:
15½" × 15½"

Designed and made by Pat Sloan

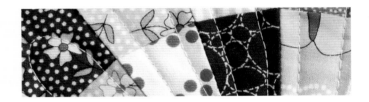

Materials

Yardage is based on 42"-wide fabric. Fat quarters are 18" × 21".

40 squares, 2½" × 2½", of assorted prints for Dresden blades
1 fat quarter of white solid for background
¼ yard of red print for binding
1 fat quarter of fabric for backing
18" × 18" piece of batting
Template plastic or EZ Dresden ruler
Glue stick

Cutting

All measurements include ¼"-wide seam allowances.

From the white solid, cut:
1 square, 15½" × 15½"

From the red print, cut:
2 strips, 2¼" × 42"

Making the Dresden Plate

1 Join two print squares to make a two-patch unit. Press the seam allowances in one direction. Make 20 units.

Make 20.

2 (Skip this step if you're using a Dresden ruler.) Trace the wedge pattern on page 197 onto template plastic, making sure to include the centerline. Cut out the wedge template, cutting directly on the line.

3 Place the wedge template on top of a two-patch unit, aligning the wider end of the template with a short, raw edge of the unit as shown. The centerline on the template should be aligned with the seamline. Carefully cut along both long edges of the template to make a wedge. Make 20 wedges.

Align. →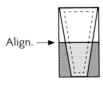

Make 20.

Dresden Ruler

If you're using a ruler, align the 4½" line on the ruler with the short, raw edge of the unit as shown. Cut along both long edges of the ruler to make a wedge. Make 20 wedges.

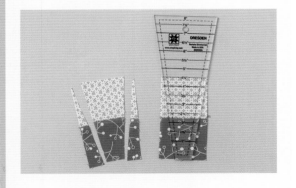

4 Fold a wedge in half lengthwise, right sides together, and sew across the wider end using a ¼" seam allowance. You can chain piece these seams to speed up the process. Trim a tiny triangle from the folded seam allowance as shown. Turn the piece right side out and use a bluntly pointed object (such as a knitting needle or chopstick) to push the tip out so it's pointy and the piece is blade shaped. Press the blade flat.

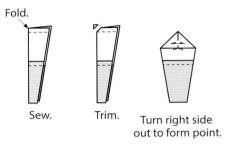

Fold.

Sew. Trim. Turn right side out to form point.

5 Repeat with all the pieces to make 20 blades.

6 Aligning the shoulders of the blades and using a ¼" seam allowance, sew 10 blades together to make a half Dresden plate. Press the seam allowances in one direction. Repeat to make a second half Dresden plate.

 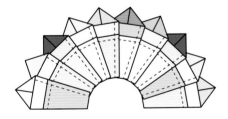

Make 2.

7 Sew the two halves together to make a ring. Press the seam allowances in one direction.

8 The center of the plate is open. To create a finished edge in the center, roll under a ¼" seam allowance. On the wrong side, use a glue stick to dab a little glue along the edge to hold the seam allowance in place.

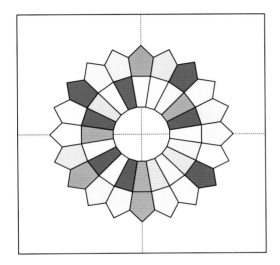

Appliquéing the Dresden Plate

1 Fold the white square in half horizontally and vertically; finger-press to establish centering lines. Unfold and use the creased lines to center the Dresden plate on the white square. Pin in place.

2 Blanket-stitch around the outer edges and the center of the Dresden plate.

Finishing the Quilt

For help with the following finishing steps, go to ShopMartingale.com/HowtoQuilt for free, illustrated instructions.

1 Layer and baste the quilt top, batting, and backing. Quilt by hand or machine. The quilt shown features a free-form quilted spiral in the center of the Dresden plate. The blades are outline stitched, and a long loop is added in the center of each blade. Bubbles add a dash of fun to the outer edges of the plate.

2 Using the red 2¼"-wide strips, prepare and attach double-fold binding.

3 Add a hanging sleeve, if desired.

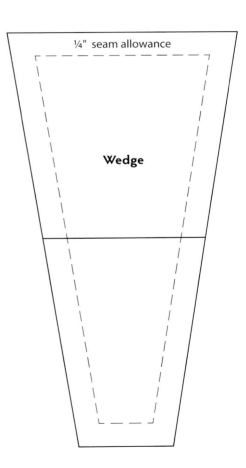

¼" seam allowance

Wedge

Friendship Star

If you're fairly new to making half-square-triangle units, Friendship Star blocks offer a wonderful opportunity to practice. By the end you'll be making them like a pro! Appliquéd circles make this quilt really shine.

Finished quilt: 40½" × 40½"
Finished block: 12" × 12"

Designed and made by Pat Sloan

Materials

Yardage is based on 42"-wide fabric.

1½ yards of cream print (fabric A) for blocks and border
¾ yard of red print (fabric B) for blocks
½ yard of green print (fabric C) for appliquéd circles and binding
1¾ yards of fabric for backing
45" × 45" piece of batting
¼ yard of paper-backed fusible web

Cutting

All measurements include ¼"-wide seam allowances.

From the cream print (fabric A), cut:
3 strips, 5" × 42"; crosscut into 18 squares, 5" × 5"
5 strips, 4½" × 42"; crosscut into 36 squares, 4½" × 4½"
2 strips, 2½" × 36½"
2 strips, 2½" × 40½"

From the red print (fabric B), cut:
3 strips, 5" × 42"; crosscut into 18 squares, 5" × 5"
2 strips, 4½" × 42"; crosscut into 9 squares, 4½" × 4½"

From the green print (fabric C), cut:
5 strips, 2¼" × 42"
Set aside the remainder of the fabric for the appliquéd circles.

From the backing fabric, cut:
1 rectangle, 40" × 45½"
1 strip, 6" × 40"
1 square, 6" × 6"

Making the Blocks

Press all seam allowances as indicated by the arrows.

1 Draw a diagonal line from corner to corner on the wrong side of each 5" fabric A square. Place a marked square on a 5" fabric B square, right sides together and raw edges aligned. Stitch ¼" from each side of the drawn line. Cut the squares apart on the marked line to make two half-square-triangle units. Trim the units to measure 4½" square. Make a total of 36 units.

Make 36 units,
4½" x 4½".

Assembling the Quilt Top

1 Lay out the blocks in three rows of three blocks each as shown in the quilt assembly diagram below. Sew the blocks together into rows. Join the rows to complete the quilt-top center, which should measure 36½" square, including seam allowances.

2 Sew the 2½" × 36½" fabric A strips to opposite sides of the quilt top. Sew the 2½" × 40½" fabric A strips to the top and bottom to complete the border. The quilt top should measure 40½" square, including seam allowances.

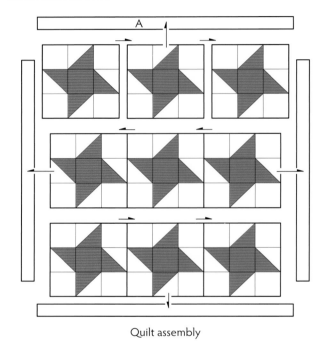

Quilt assembly

2 Lay out four half-square-triangle units, four 4½" fabric A squares, and one 4½" fabric B square in three rows, rotating the half-square-triangle units as shown.

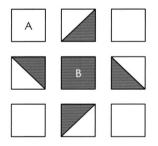

3 Sew the pieces together into rows. Join the rows to complete a Friendship Star block. The block should measure 12½" square, including seam allowances. Make a total of nine blocks.

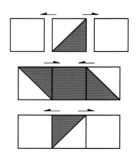
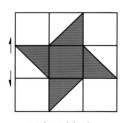

Make 9 blocks,
12½" x 12½".

Adding the Appliquéd Dots

Visit ShopMartingale.com/HowtoQuilt for complete instructions about fusible appliqué and a variety of other techniques.

1 Using the dot pattern on page 201, trace 13 dots onto the fusible web. Roughly cut out each shape, about ½" beyond the drawn line.

2 Position the fusible-web dots on the wrong side of the reversed fabric C. Fuse as instructed by the manufacturer. Cut out the dots on the marked lines. Remove the paper backing from each dot.

3 Place a dot in the center of each block. Center a dot atop the seam intersections as shown in the quilt photo on page 200. Fuse the appliqués in place. Straight stitch around the outer edges of each dot using matching thread.

Finishing the Quilt

For help with the following finishing steps, go to ShopMartingale.com/HowtoQuilt for free, illustrated instructions.

1 To make the backing, sew the 6" square to one end of the 6" × 40" strip to make a strip that's 6" × 45½". Sew the strip to the long side of the 40" × 45½" rectangle to make a backing that measures 45½" square.

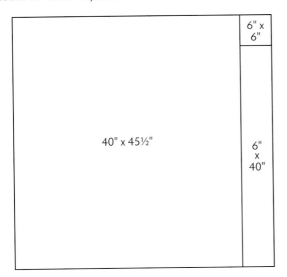

Make a 45½" square backing.

2 Layer and baste the quilt top, batting, and backing. Quilt by hand or machine. The quilt shown is machine quilted using cream thread around each star shape and in an allover grid pattern in the background. Red thread is used to stitch straight lines from point to point through each Friendship Star block.

3 Using the 2¼"-wide fabric C strips, prepare and attach double-fold binding.

4 Add a hanging sleeve, if desired.

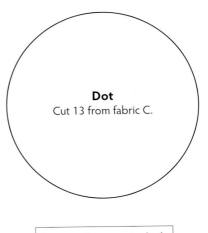

Dot
Cut 13 from fabric C.

Pattern does not include seam allowance.

Hanging Around

Wreaths are a cherished, traditional part of holiday decorating, but they certainly don't have to be ornate or stodgy. This simple, modern wreath is ready to grace the table, and the center is left plain so you can add a festive centerpiece!

Finished table topper:
28½" × 28½"

Designed and made by Cindy Lammon

Materials

Yardage is based on 42"-wide fabric.

1⅛ yards of white solid for background
½ yard *total* of assorted green prints for piecing
⅓ yard of red-and-white stripe for binding
1⅛ yards of fabric for backing
34" × 34" piece of batting

Cutting

All measurements include ¼"-wide seam allowances.

From the white solid, cut:
1 strip, 12½" × 42"; crosscut into 1 square, 12½" × 12½".
   Trim the remainder of the strip to 4½" wide;
   crosscut into 4 rectangles, 4½" × 6½".
3 strips, 3" × 42"; crosscut into 30 squares, 3" × 3".
   Cut in half diagonally to yield 60 triangles.
1 strip, 4½" × 42"; crosscut into 12 rectangles,
   2½" × 4½"
2 strips, 2½" × 24½"
2 strips, 2½" × 28½"

From the assorted green prints, cut a *total* of:
4 squares, 4½" × 4½"
30 squares, 3" × 3"; cut in half diagonally to yield
   60 triangles

From the red-and-white stripe, cut:
3 strips, 2½" × 42"

Making the Blocks

Press all seam allowances as indicated by the arrows.

1 Draw a diagonal line from corner to corner on the wrong side of the green 4½" squares. Place a marked square on each corner of the white 12½" square, noting the direction of the marked lines. Sew on the marked line. Trim ¼" from the stitching line; press.

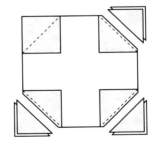 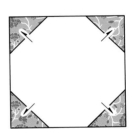

2 Sew a green triangle to a white triangle along the long edges. Repeat to make a total of 60 half-square-triangle units. Trim the units to 2½" square, including seam allowances.

Make 60.

3 Sew six half-square-triangle units together as shown to make row A. Repeat to make a total of eight rows.

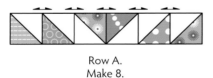

Row A.
Make 8.

4 Sew two half-square-triangle units together as shown. Sew a white 2½" × 4½" rectangle to each end to make row B. Repeat to make a total of four rows.

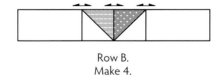

Row B.
Make 4.

5 Sew two A rows and one B row together as shown. Repeat to make a total of four side units.

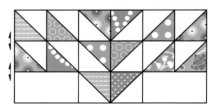

Make 4.

6 Sew one of the remaining half-square-triangle units to a white 2½" × 4½" rectangle. Sew a white 4½" × 6½" rectangle to the bottom of this unit. Repeat to make a total of four corner units.

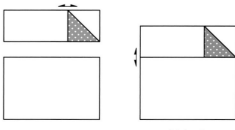

Make 4.

Assembling the Quilt Top

1 Refer to the assembly diagram below to arrange the side units and corner units into three horizontal rows. Sew the units in each row together, and then join the rows.

2 Sew the white 2½" × 24½" strips to the sides of the quilt top. Sew the white 2½" × 28½" strips to the top and bottom of the quilt top.

Finishing the Quilt

For help with the following finishing steps, go to ShopMartingale.com/HowtoQuilt for free, illustrated instructions.

1 Layer and baste the quilt top, batting, and backing. Quilt by hand or machine.

2 Using the red-and-white 2½"-wide strips, prepare and attach double-fold binding.

3 Add a hanging sleeve, if desired.

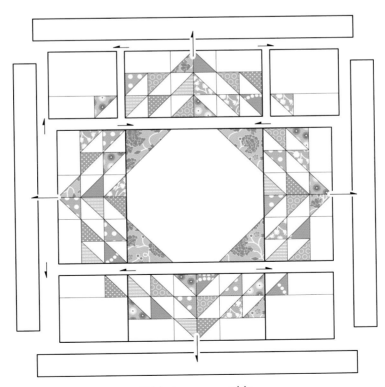

Table-topper assembly

Birdsong

They may not be partridges in a pear tree, but these simple-to-stitch feathered friends will add a tuneful note to your holiday table. Patchwork Star blocks and a wide outer border show off prints scattered with holiday foliage.

Finished quilt: 34½" × 34½"
Finished block: 8" × 8"

Designed and made by Gail Pan

Materials

Yardage is based on 42"-wide fabric unless otherwise noted.

⅓ yard of cream tone on tone for embroidery background

⅝ yard of green dot for Star blocks, inner border, and binding

½ yard of cream print for Star blocks

⅞ yard of red print for Star blocks and outer border

1⅛ yards of fabric for backing

38" × 38" piece of batting

⅝ yard of lightweight fusible interfacing, 18" to 20" wide, for embroidery backing

6-strand embroidery floss in dark green, light green, red, and yellow

Size 8 pearl cotton in ecru

¼" quilter's tape (optional)

Cutting

All measurements include ¼"-wide seam allowances.

From the cream tone on tone, cut:
4 squares, 9" × 9"

From the lightweight fusible interfacing, cut:
4 squares, 9" × 9"

From the green dot, cut:
5 strips, 2½" × 42"; crosscut *1 of the strips* into:
- 4 squares, 2½" × 2½"
- 4 rectangles, 2½" × 4½"
4 strips, 1½" × 42"; crosscut into:
- 2 strips, 1½" × 24½"
- 2 strips, 1½" × 26½"

From the cream print, cut:
1 strip, 4½" × 42"; crosscut into 5 squares, 4½" × 4½"
3 strips, 2½" × 42"; crosscut into 40 squares, 2½" × 2½"

From the red print, cut:
3 strips, 2½" × 42"; crosscut into:
- 16 squares, 2½" × 2½"
- 16 rectangles, 2½" × 4½"
4 strips, 4½" × 42"; crosscut into:
- 2 strips, 4½" × 26½"
- 2 strips, 4½" × 34½"

Embroidering the Designs

For help with basic hand-embroidery stitches, go to ShopMartingale.com/HowtoQuilt for free downloadable information.

1 Using the pattern on page 210, trace the Birdsong design onto the right side of each cream 9" square. Fuse a square of interfacing to the wrong side of each marked square.

Making the Blocks

Press all seam allowances as indicated by the arrows.

1 Mark a diagonal line on the wrong side of eight cream-print 2½" squares. Aligning the corners, pin a marked square on one end of a green rectangle, right sides together. Sew directly on the marked line. Trim ¼" from the seamline and press. Repeat on the opposite end of the rectangle to make a flying-geese unit. Make four units.

Make 4.

2 Using two strands of floss, embroider the designs, following the embroidery key and color guides on the pattern.

3 Gently press the stitched squares. Centering the embroidered design and aligning the 45° line on your ruler with the tree trunk, trim the squares to 8½" × 8½". Set aside.

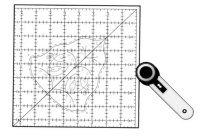

2 Lay out the flying-geese units from step 1, four green squares, and one cream-print 4½" square as shown. Sew the pieces together into rows. Sew the rows together to make one green Star block.

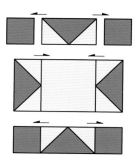 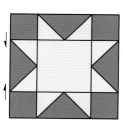

Make 1.

3 Repeat steps 1 and 2 to make four Star blocks using red print.

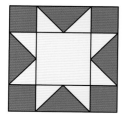

Make 4.

Assembling the Quilt Top

1 Lay out the Star blocks and the embroidered squares in three rows as shown. Sew the blocks and squares together into rows. Sew the rows together. The quilt top should measure 24½" square.

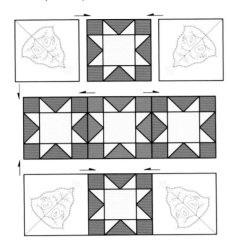

2 Sew the green 24½"-long strips to opposite sides of the quilt top. Sew the green 26½"-long strips to the top and bottom of the quilt top.

3 Sew the red 26½"-long strips to opposite sides of the quilt top. Sew the red 34½"-long strips to the top and bottom of the quilt top.

Quilt assembly

Finishing the Quilt

For help with the following finishing steps, go to ShopMartingale.com/HowtoQuilt for free, illustrated instructions.

1 Layer and baste the quilt top, batting, and backing. Quilt by hand or machine. The quilt shown is quilted using pearl cotton and big-stitch quilting ¼" inside the squares and triangles in the Star blocks and ¼" from the seamline in the inner and outer borders.

Quilting Tip

Attach the binding before quilting ¼" from the binding seam. That way the quilting line will be exactly ¼" from the seamline.

2 Using the green dot 2½"-wide strips, prepare and attach double-fold binding.

3 Add a hanging sleeve, if desired.

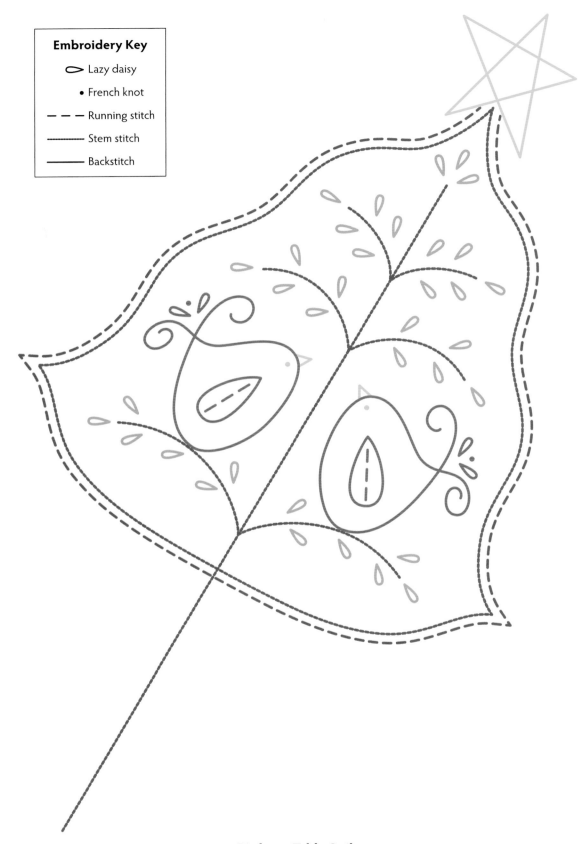

Embroidery Key

◯ Lazy daisy

• French knot

– – – Running stitch

••••••••• Stem stitch

——— Backstitch

Birdsong Table Quilt

Merry Christmas to All

Santa's flying over the rooftops with his Merry Christmas banner in this colorful, easily stitched design. A patchwork of embroidered borders and a topsy-turvy Christmas-tree print add to the charm of this folk-art holiday hanging.

Finished quilt:
8½" × 12"

Designed and made by Robin Kingsley

Materials

Yardage is based on 42"-wide fabric. Fat quarters are 18" × 21".

1 fat quarter of tan dot for embroidery backgrounds
1 fat quarter of tree print for borders and backing
⅛ yard of red dot for binding
11" × 14" piece of batting
Size 8 pearl cotton in ecru, red, gold, green, blue, golden brown, and dark brown
Jute twine for hanging loops
Rustic twig OR vintage cotton-mill spool*

*Find a lichen-covered twig about 10" long or purchase a spool once used in a cotton mill to use as a hanger for your embroidery.

Cutting

All measurements include ¼"-wide seam allowances.

From the tan dot, cut:
1 rectangle, 14" × 16"

From the tree print, cut:
2 strips, 1¾" × 8½"
1 rectangle, 10" × 13"

From the red dot, cut:
2 strips, 2" × 42"

Embroidering the Designs

For help with basic hand-embroidery stitches, go to ShopMartingale.com/HowtoQuilt for free downloadable information.

1 Transfer the designs (page 215) to the tan rectangle, leaving at least 2" of space between designs.

Perfect Palette

Thread each color of pearl cotton on a different needle so that you can switch between colors with ease.

2 Referring to the photographs, stitch the design in the colors shown in the pattern. Follow the stitch details in the box on page 214. Vary the length of backstitches to suit the design, using shorter stitches around tight curves and lettering.

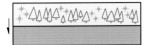

2 Sew one tree-print 1¾" × 8½" strip to the bottom of the Tiny Trees border. Sew the second tree-print strip to the top of the Houses border.

3 Stitch the Tiny Trees unit to the top of the Santa panel and add the Houses unit to the bottom of the Santa panel.

3 If you used water-soluble stabilizer to transfer the designs, rinse the embroidery thoroughly in running water to remove the stabilizer.

4 Wash the embroidery if necessary in sudsy water and rinse thoroughly. Dry the work flat. Lay the finished embroidery face down on a towel and press it from the wrong side with a steam iron. Use a bit of spray starch to give the embroidery a crisp feel.

Assembling the Quilt Top

Press all seam allowances as indicated by the arrows.

1 Trim the Tiny Trees and Houses borders to measure 2" × 8½". Trim the Santa panel to 6½" × 8½". Keep all of the designs centered as you trim.

Finishing the Quilt

For help with the following finishing steps, go to ShopMartingale.com/HowtoQuilt for free, illustrated instructions.

1 Layer and baste the quilt top, batting, and backing. Quilt by hand or machine. The quilt shown is quilted with ecru pearl cotton and running-stitch quilting ⅛" inside each embroidered section, along the border seams.

2 Using the red dot 2"-wide strips, prepare and attach double-fold binding.

3 Cut two 8" pieces of jute twine. Fold one piece in half and tie a large overhand knot near the ends, leaving a 2½" loop. Trim the ends near the knot. Make two.

Color and Stitch Placement

TINY TREES BORDER

- **Treetops:** green backstitch
- **Tree trunks:** golden brown backstitch
- **Stars:** with blue, make a large cross-stitch with horizontal and vertical legs, then stitch a smaller cross-stitch over its center. Add French knots (wrapped once) to the ends of the longest stitches.

HOUSES BORDER

- **Houses:** dark brown backstitch
- **Chimneys:** red backstitch
- **Doors:** backstitch; add cross-stitch at the center of each. Use green for houses 1 and 5; red for houses 2 and 4; and blue for houses 3 and 6.
- **Windows:** gold backstitch
- **Treetops:** green backstitch
- **Tree trunks:** golden brown backstitch
- **Stars:** with blue, make a large cross-stitch with horizontal and vertical legs, then stitch a smaller cross-stitch over its center. Add French knots (wrapped once) to the ends of the longest stitches.

SANTA PANEL

- **Santa's suit and hat:** red backstitch
- **Santa's beard, mustache, hat and sleeve cuffs, and pom-pom:** ecru backstitch
- **Treetops, Santa's mittens, and pine branch:** green backstitch
- **Tree trunks:** golden brown backstitch
- **Letters:** red backstitch; add a French knot (wrapped once) for the dot over the i
- **Candy cane, peppermint stick, chimney, Santa's mouth, and backpack patch and strap:** red backstitch; add a French knot (wrapped twice) to the strap
- **Details on cuffs:** red running stitch
- **Trim on Santa's robe:** with blue, make a large cross-stitch with horizontal and vertical legs, then stitch a smaller cross-stitch over its center. Add French knots (wrapped once) to the ends of the longest stitches.
- **Star, buckle, and door:** gold backstitch
- **Backpack detail:** gold cross-stitch
- **Santa's eyes:** dark brown satin stitch (just three or four stitches per eye)
- **Santa's eyebrows:** dark brown straight stitch
- **Santa's nose, belt, boots, house, banner outline, fringe, ribbons flowing from star:** dark brown backstitch. Add French knots (wrapped twice) and lazy daisy loops as you come to them in these areas.

4 Position the hanging loops 2" from the side edges of the wall hanging, with the knots just below the binding. Thread a needle with ecru pearl cotton and take several stitches over the jute, just above the knot, to secure the hanging loop to the wall hanging. Bury the thread tails between the project's layers.

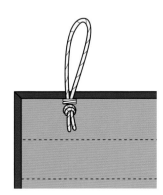

French knot
(1 wrap)

Merry Christmas to ALL

Straight stitch

Cross-stitch

Lazy daisy

Running stitch

French knot
(1 wrap)

Allow 2" between designs
when tracing onto fabric.

Embroidery Key

—— Backstitch	● French knot	- - - Running stitch
✕✕ Cross-stitch	◯ Lazy daisy	■ Satin stitch
		— Straight stitch

Seeing Stars

When you find a bold and beautiful novelty print, don't you want to show it off?
Make your focus fabric the star by placing it right in the center, and think outside
the holiday-decor box by replacing traditional pine green with refreshing teal.

Finished quilt: 40½" × 40½"
Finished block: 8" × 8"

Designed and made by Cindy Lammon

Materials

Yardage is based on 42"-wide fabric.

⅝ yard of white solid for background
½ yard of teal tone on tone for star points
¼ yard of teal-and-red stripe for star centers
¼ yard of red print for alternate block centers
⅝ yard of large-scale print for center square
⅝ yard of teal-and-red print for border*
½ yard of red solid for binding
2 yards of fabric for pieced backing
46" × 46" piece of batting

*Be sure your fabric is at least 41" wide after washing.
If not, purchase ¾ yard.

Cutting

All measurements include ¼"-wide seam allowances.

From the white solid, cut:
3 strips, 4½" × 42"; crosscut into 48 rectangles,
    2½" × 4½"
2 strips, 2½" × 42"; crosscut into 32 squares,
    2½" × 2½"

From the teal tone on tone, cut:
6 strips, 2½" × 42"; crosscut into 96 squares,
    2½" × 2½"

From the teal-and-red stripe, cut:
1 strip, 4½" × 42"; crosscut into 8 squares, 4½" × 4½"

From the red print, cut:
1 strip, 4½" × 42"; crosscut into 8 squares, 4½" × 4½"

From the large-scale print, cut:
1 square, 16½" × 16½"

From the teal-and-red print, cut:
4 strips, 4½" × 42"

From the backing fabric, cut:
1 rectangle, 40½" × 48½"
2 rectangles, 8½" × 24½"

From the red solid, cut:
5 strips, 2½" × 42"

the rows to complete the block. Repeat to make a total of eight Star blocks. Set the remaining flying-geese units aside for the alternate blocks.

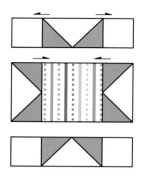 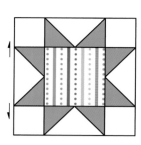

Make 8.

Making the Alternate Blocks

Sew two of the remaining flying-geese units to opposite sides of a red 4½" square. Repeat to make a total of eight alternate blocks.

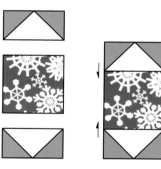

Make 8.

Making the Star Blocks

Press all seam allowances as indicated by the arrows.

1 Draw a diagonal line from corner to corner on the wrong side of the teal tone-on-tone 2½" squares. Place a marked square on one end of a white 2½" × 4½" rectangle, right sides together. Sew on the drawn line. Trim ¼" from the stitching line, and press toward the resulting teal triangle. Repeat on the other end of the rectangle. Make 48 flying-geese units.

Make 48.

2 Arrange four flying-geese units from step 1, one teal-and-red striped 4½" square, and four white 2½" squares into three horizontal rows as shown above right. Sew the pieces in each row together. Join

Assembling the Quilt Top

1 Sew two alternate blocks and one Star block together as shown. Repeat to make a total of two rows.

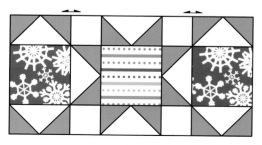

Make 2.

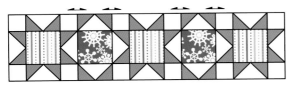

2 Sew three Star blocks and two alternate blocks together as shown. Repeat to make a total of two rows.

Make 2.

3 Refer to the assembly diagram below to sew the rows from step 1 to opposite sides of the large-scale print 16½" square. Sew the rows from step 2 to the top and bottom of the square.

4 Trim two teal-and-red print 4½"-wide strips to the length of the quilt top and sew them to the sides of the quilt top. Trim the remaining two teal-and-red print strips to the width of the quilt top and sew them to the top and bottom of the quilt top.

Quilt assembly

Finishing the Quilt

For help with the following finishing steps, go to ShopMartingale.com/HowtoQuilt for free, illustrated instructions.

1 Sew the backing pieces together as shown.

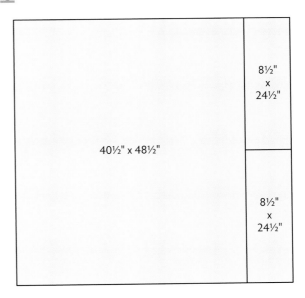

8½" x 24½"

40½" x 48½"

8½" x 24½"

2 Layer and baste the quilt top, batting, and backing. Quilt by hand or machine.

3 Using the red-solid 2½"-wide strips, prepare and attach double-fold binding.

4 Add a hanging sleeve, if desired.

keep Christmas in
your heart ♥♥ and
home, all year long

Heart and Home

Decorate your home and warm your heart with this whimsical combination of embroidery and patchwork. The assorted squares and rectangles represent a merry mix of prints, from checks and polka dots to stars and holly sprigs.

Finished quilt:
23½" × 24½"

Designed and made by Gail Pan

Materials

Yardage is based on 42"-wide fabric unless otherwise noted. Fat quarters are 18"×21".

1 fat quarter of cream fabric for embroidery backgrounds
⅓ yard *total* of assorted prints for squares and rectangles
⅜ yard of red star print for border
⅓ yard of green print for binding
¾ yard of fabric for backing
26" × 27" piece of batting
⅝ yard of lightweight fusible interfacing, 18" to 20" wide, for embroidery backing
6-strand embroidery floss in red

Cutting

All measurements include ¼"-wide seam allowances.

From the cream fabric, cut:
1 rectangle, 8" × 10"
1 rectangle, 5" × 9"
1 square, 4" × 4"
1 rectangle, 4" × 7"

From the lightweight fusible interfacing, cut:
1 rectangle, 8" × 10"
1 rectangle, 5" × 9"
1 square, 4" × 4"
1 rectangle, 4" × 7"

From the assorted prints, cut a *total* of:
27 squares, 2½" × 2½"
11 rectangles, 2½" × 3½"
2 rectangles, 1½" × 3½"
1 rectangle, 1½" × 4½"

From the red star print, cut:
3 strips, 3½" × 42"; crosscut into:
- 2 strips, 3½" × 18½"
- 2 strips, 3½" × 23½"

From the green print, cut:
3 strips, 2½" × 42"

Embroidering the Designs

For help with basic hand-embroidery stitches, go to ShopMartingale.com/HowtoQuilt for free downloadable information.

1 Using the patterns on pages 224 and 225, trace the House design onto the right side of the cream 8" × 10" rectangle. Trace the Tree design onto the right side of the cream 5" × 9" rectangle. Trace the Heart design onto the right side of the cream 4" square. Trace the Saying design onto the right side of the cream 4" × 7" rectangle. Fuse the interfacing pieces to the wrong side of each marked rectangle and square.

2 Using two strands of floss, embroider the designs, following the embroidery keys on the patterns.

Assembling the Wall Hanging

Press all seam allowances as indicated by the arrows.

1 Centering the embroidered designs, trim the House block to 7½" × 9½", the Tree block to 4½" × 8½", the Heart block to 3½" × 3½", and the Saying block to 3½" × 6½".

2 Sew a print 1½" × 3½" rectangle to the left of the Saying block. Join two print 2½" squares and a print 2½" × 3½" rectangle to make a strip. Sew the strip to the top of the Saying block. Sew the House block to the top of the pieced strip.

 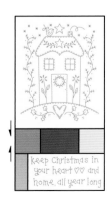

3 Sew a print 1½" × 3½" rectangle to the right of the Heart block; then sew a print 1½" × 4½" rectangle to the top of the Heart block. Join two print 2½" squares and sew them to the bottom of the Heart block. Sew the Tree block to the bottom of the two-square strip.

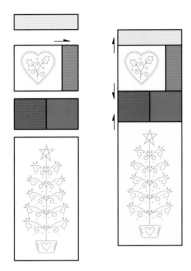

4 Sew together four print 2½" squares and two print 2½" × 3½" rectangles to make a strip.

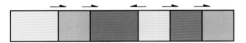

5 Lay out the sections from steps 2 and 3; place the strip from step 4 between the sections. Join the sections and center strip.

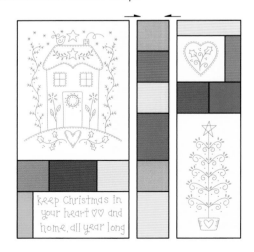

Adding the Borders

Refer to the assembly diagram at right as needed throughout.

1 Join five print 2½" squares and one print 2½" × 3½" rectangle to make the top border. Sew the border to the top of the center block.

2 Join five print 2½" squares and two print 2½" × 3½" rectangles to make the left side border. Sew the border to the left side of the center block.

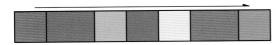

3 Join two print 2½" × 3½" rectangles and five print 2½" squares to make the right side border. Sew the border to the right side of the center block.

4 Join three print 2½" × 3½" rectangles and four print 2½" squares to make the bottom border. Sew the border to the bottom of the block.

5 Sew the red star-print 18½"-long strips to the sides of the wall-hanging top. Sew the red star-print 23½"-long strips to the top and bottom of the wall hanging.

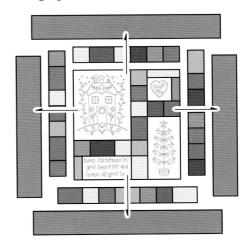

Wall-hanging assembly

Finishing the Wall Hanging

For help with the following finishing steps, go to ShopMartingale.com/HowtoQuilt for free, illustrated instructions.

1 Layer and baste the quilt top, batting, and backing. Quilt by hand or machine. The quilt shown is machine quilted using a meandering design of stars, hearts, and holly leaves. A holly design is quilted in the border.

2 Using the green 2½"-wide strips, prepare and attach double-fold binding.

3 Add a hanging sleeve, if desired.

Embroidery Key

◯ Lazy daisy

• French knot

– – – Running stitch

——— Backstitch

Heart and Home

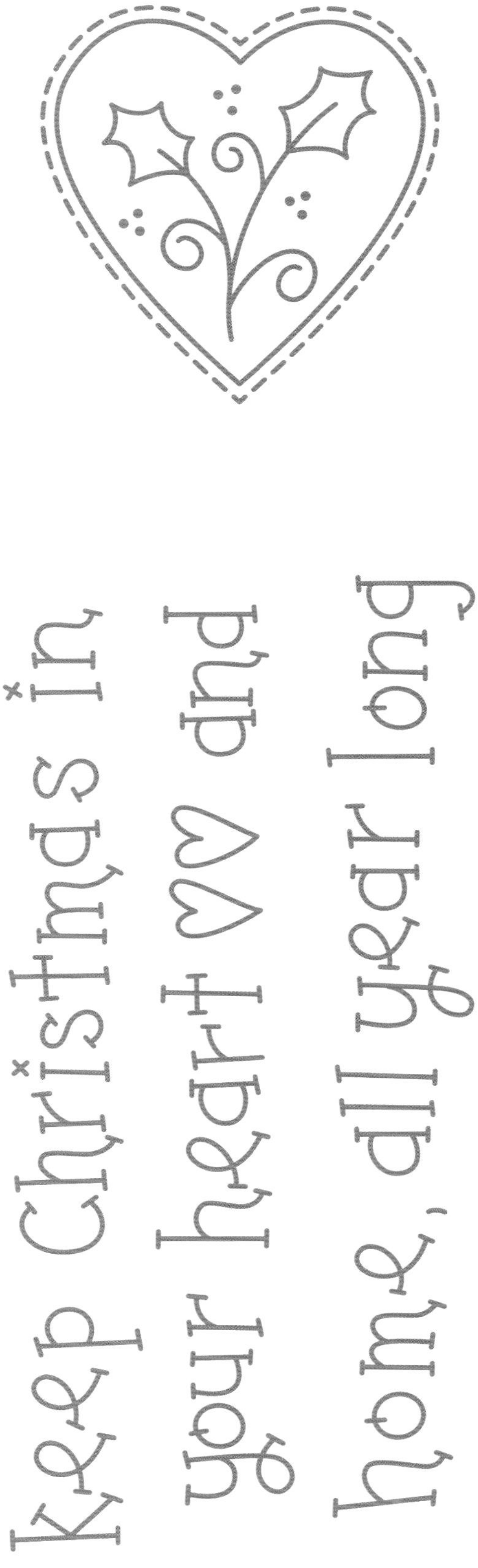
Keep Christmas in
your heart ♥ and
home, all year long

Embroidery Key

- Lazy daisy
- French knot
- Cross-stitch
- Running stitch
- Backstitch

Heart and Home

Portraits of Santa

Santa Claus has many charming looks, and this little quilt shows off four portraits of the jolly fellow, each framed in an embroidered redwork square. Additional decorative embroidery stitches enliven the simple pieced border.

Finished quilt:
16" × 16"

Designed and made by Gail Pan

Materials

Yardage is based on 42"-wide fabric.

¼ yard of cream dot for embroidery backgrounds
¾ yard of red tone on tone for border, backing,
   and binding
⅛ yard of red dot for border
18" × 18" piece of batting
Size 8 pearl cotton in red and cream
Paper for foundation piecing
1 red square button, 1⅛" wide
1 red round button, ⅞" diameter

Cutting

All measurements include ¼"-wide seam allowances.

From the cream dot, cut:
4 squares, 8" × 8"

From the red tone on tone, cut:
4 strips, 1¼" × 42"
1 strip, 1¼" × 12"
1 square, 18" × 18"
2 strips, 2" × 42"

From the red dot, cut:
2 strips, 1¼" × 42"
2 strips, 1¼" × 12"

Embroidering the Designs

For help with basic hand-embroidery stitches, go to ShopMartingale.com/HowtoQuilt for free downloadable information.

1 Transfer one of the designs (pages 230 and 231) to each cream square, centering the placement.

2 Using red pearl cotton and referring to the photographs, stitch the main design lines with a backstitch. Vary the length of the stitches, using shorter stitches along tight curves such as jingle bells and letters. Stitch the dots with French knots, wrapping the thread around the needle twice. Use a running stitch for the broken lines, lazy daisies for the loops, straight stitches for short lines, and a cross-stitch where there is an X on the design. Stitch the oval eyes with three or four small satin stitches, and fill the noses (except the Santa at lower left) with satin stitches.

3 If you used water-soluble stabilizer to transfer the designs, rinse the embroidery thoroughly in running water to remove the stabilizer.

4 Wash the embroidery if necessary in sudsy water and rinse thoroughly. Dry the work flat. Lay the finished embroidery face down on a towel and press it from the wrong side with a steam iron. Use a bit of spray starch to give the embroidery a crisp feel.

Making the Borders

1 Sew a red-dot 1¼" × 42" strip between two red tone-on-tone 1¼" × 42" strips to make a strip set; make two. Crosscut the strip sets into four border segments, 2¾" × 11½", and four corner segments, 2¾" × 1¼".

Make 2 strip sets.
Cut 4 of each segment.

2 Sew the red tone-on-tone 1¼" × 12" strip between the two red-dot 1¼" × 12" strips. Crosscut the strip set into eight corner segments, 2¾" × 1¼".

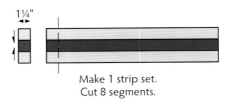

Make 1 strip set.
Cut 8 segments.

3 Sew a corner segment from step 1 between two corner segments from step 2 to make a Nine Patch block, 2¾" square. Make four.

Make 4.

Assembling the Center Unit

Press all seam allowances as indicated by the arrows.

1 Trim each embroidered square to measure 6" × 6", keeping the design centered.

2 Arrange the four Santas as shown in the photographs. Sew the embroidered blocks together in pairs to form two rows and then join the rows, matching the intersecting seams. The unit will measure 11½" square.

3 With cream pearl cotton, embroider across the seams between blocks with a herringbone stitch.

4 Stitch a border segment to the top of the center unit. Sew a second border segment to the bottom of the embroidered center.

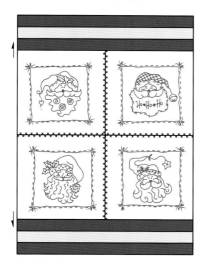

5 Stitch a Nine Patch block to each end of the remaining border segments, matching the intersecting seams, to make the side borders.

Make 2.

6 Sew the side borders to the table topper.

Finishing the Quilt

For help with the following finishing steps, go to ShopMartingale.com/HowtoQuilt for free, illustrated instructions.

1 Layer and baste the quilt top, batting, and red 18" backing square. Quilt by hand or machine. The quilt shown is quilted using cream pearl cotton and running-stitch quilting on the cream fabric, just inside the border seams. A feather stitch with red pearl cotton is quilted along the center of each red-dot strip in the borders.

2 Stack the two buttons and sew them to the center of the quilt as a unit.

Button Up

Vary the size, shape, and quantity of the buttons as you like. Use a single button, or stack two or more as in the quilt shown on page 228.

3 Using the red tone-on-tone 2"-wide strips, prepare and attach double-fold binding.

4 Add a hanging sleeve, if desired.

Top left

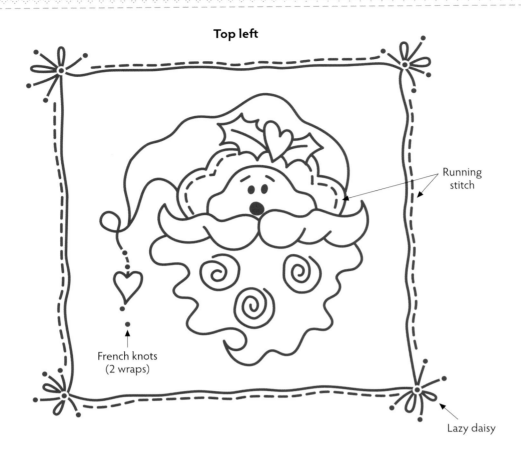

Running stitch

French knots
(2 wraps)

Lazy daisy

Bottom left

Satin stitch

Embroidery Key

———— Backstitch

✕✕ Cross-stitch

• French knot

⬯ Lazy daisy

- - - Running stitch

■ Satin stitch

— Straight stitch

Top right

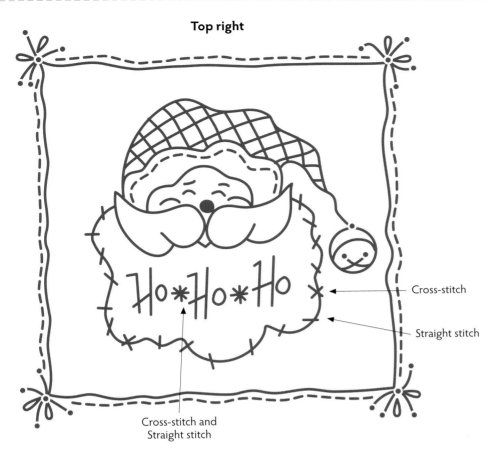

Cross-stitch

Straight stitch

Cross-stitch and
Straight stitch

Bottom right

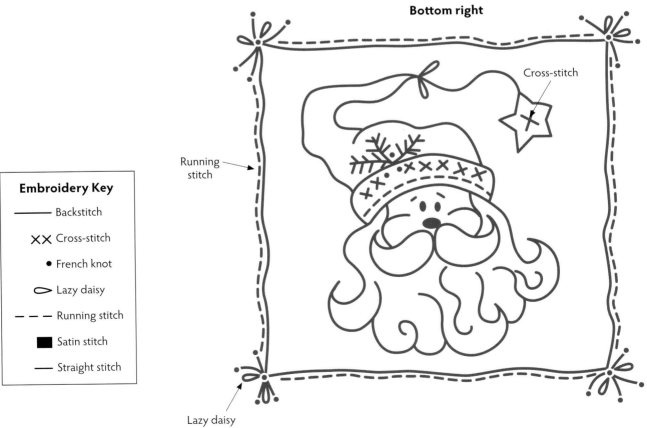

Cross-stitch

Running
stitch

Embroidery Key

——	Backstitch
✕✕	Cross-stitch
●	French knot
◯	Lazy daisy
– – –	Running stitch
■	Satin stitch
—	Straight stitch

Lazy daisy

Tiny Trees

When dressing up your home for the season, don't overlook your sewing space! This unfussy mini-quilt goes together so quickly, you may want to make another one and turn it into a festive companion throw pillow.

Finished quilt: 18½" × 18½"
Finished block: 3" × 3"

Designed and made by Christa Watson

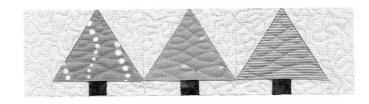

Materials

Yardage is based on 42"-wide fabric.

⅛ yard of brown print for tree trunks
⅝ yard of cream print for background*
¼ yard *total* of assorted green prints for trees
¼ yard of mint green print for binding
24" × 24" square of fabric for backing
22" × 22" square of batting
Paper for foundation piecing

*For best results, choose a nondirectional fabric for the background.

Cutting

All measurements include ¼"-wide seam allowances. Fabric pieces are cut generously for paper piecing. Label all pieces to keep them organized.

From the brown print, cut:
1 strip, 1½" × 42"; crosscut into 15 squares, 1½" × 1½" (piece 1)

From the cream print, cut:
1 strip, 3½" × 42"; crosscut into:
- 2 rectangles, 3½" × 6½"
- 2 rectangles, 3½" × 5"
- 2 squares, 3½" × 3½"
- 2 rectangles, 2" × 3½"

3 strips, 2¼" × 42"; crosscut into 30 rectangles, 2¼" × 4" (pieces 5 and 6)
4 strips, 2" × 42"; crosscut into:
- 2 strips, 2" × 19"
- 2 strips, 2" × 16"
- 30 rectangles, 1½" × 2" (pieces 2 and 3)

From the assorted green prints, cut:
15 squares, 4" × 4" (piece 4)

From the mint green print, cut:
2 strips, 2½" × 42"

Making the Blocks

For more details on paper-foundation piecing, go to ShopMartingale.com/HowtoQuilt for free downloadable information.

1 Make 15 copies of the Tree block foundation on page 235.

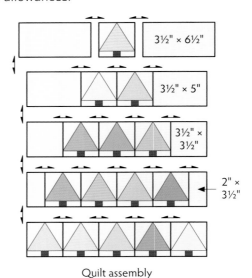

2 Sew the pieces into rows; join the rows. The quilt center should measure 15½" square, including seam allowances.

3½" × 6½"

3½" × 5"

3½" × 3½"

2" × 3½"

Quilt assembly

2 Foundation piece in the following order, beginning with piece 1 and the brown print. Make 15 paper-pieced Tree blocks.
- **Piece 1:** brown print
- **Pieces 2 and 3:** cream print
- **Piece 4:** green print
- **Pieces 5 and 6:** cream print

3 The blocks should measure 3½" square, including seam allowances.

Make 15 blocks, 3½" × 3½".

Assembling the Quilt Top

Press all seam allowances as indicated by the arrows.

1 Lay out the Tree blocks and cream background squares and rectangles in five rows as shown in the quilt assembly diagram at right.

3 Measure the length of the quilt center. Trim the cream 2" × 16" strips to this measurement. Sew the strips to the sides of the pieced quilt center.

4 Measure the width of the quilt, including the just-added borders. Trim the cream 2" × 19" strips to this measurement. Sew the strips to the top and bottom of the quilt.

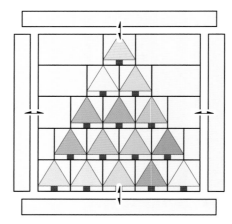

Adding borders

Finishing the Quilt

For help with the following finishing steps, go to ShopMartingale.com/HowtoQuilt for free, illustrated instructions.

1 Layer and baste the quilt top, batting, and backing. Quilt by hand or machine. The quilt shown is quilted with a continuous design of cursive capital *L*s in each of the trees and a simple stipple in the background.

2 Using the mint green 2½"-wide strips, prepare and attach double-fold binding.

3 Add a hanging sleeve, if desired.

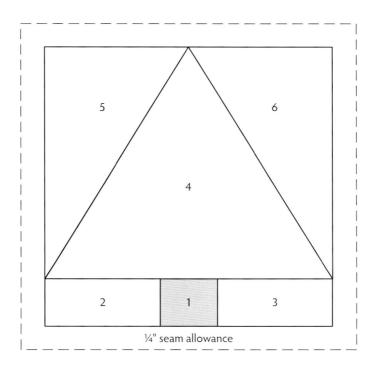

¼" seam allowance

I'm A Little Snowman
Short and Fat
Here is my Broomstick
Here is my Hat!

Little Snowman

A grinning snowman decked out in a top hat poses in the garden with a friendly bird companion, a perfect pair stitched above a fun little verse that's just right for winter. The carrot-button nose and glass-bead buttons can be embroidered instead.

Finished quilt:
7" × 11½"

Designed and made by Robin Kingsley

Materials

Yardage is based on 42"-wide fabric. Fat quarters are 18"×21".

1 fat quarter of cream tone on tone for embroidery
    background
⅛ yard of dark blue tone on tone for piecing and
    binding
¼ yard of blue print #1 for piecing and backing
⅛ yard of blue print #2 for piecing
⅛ yard of dark blue print for piecing
⅛ yard of blue dot for piecing
8" × 12" piece of batting
Size 8 pearl cotton in blue, orange, and ecru
4 blue glass beads, size 8 (optional)
1 carrot button, ⅝" long (optional)
1 snowman button, 1" tall (optional)

Cutting

All measurements include ¼"-wide seam allowances.

From the cream tone on tone, cut:
1 rectangle, 8" × 11"

From the dark blue tone on tone, cut:
1 strip, 2" × 42"*
2 rectangles, ¾" × 7½"
2 rectangles, ¾" × 5"

From blue print #1, cut:
1 rectangle, 7" × 11½"
1 rectangle, 1½" × 8"
1 rectangle, 1" × 7"

From blue print #2, cut:
1 rectangle, 1½" × 8"
1 rectangle, 1" × 7"

From the dark blue print, cut:
1 rectangle, 1½" × 7"
1 rectangle, 1" × 7"

From the blue dot, cut:
1 rectangle, 1½" × 7"

From the batting, cut:
1 rectangle, 7" × 11½"

*If your fabric is narrow, you may need to cut an additional partial 2"-wide strip to complete the binding.

Embroidering the Design

For help with basic hand-embroidery stitches, go to ShopMartingale.com/HowtoQuilt for free downloadable information.

1 Transfer the design (page 240) to the center of the cream rectangle. If you're using a button for the carrot nose, don't trace the nose onto the fabric.

2 Referring to the quilt photo on page 236 and the embroidery key on page 240, stitch the main design lines with backstitches. Vary the stitch length as needed, using shorter stitches along tight curves and letters. Stitch the short, straight lines with straight stitches, the X shapes with cross-stitches, and the broken lines with running stitches. Satin stitch the snowman's eyes and use French knots, wrapped twice, for the berries on the branch. The bird's eye and the dot over each letter *i* are sewn with a single, tiny straight stitch.

3 If you're omitting the beads, stitch a French knot at each button location and embroider the carrot-shaped nose with satin stitches in orange pearl cotton. If you prefer a more dimensional appearance, omit the embroidery and attach the carrot button at the nose location. Take two stitches through each glass bead to secure it to the snowman.

4 Wash the embroidery if necessary in sudsy water and rinse thoroughly. Dry the work flat. Press the finished embroidery from the wrong side with a steam iron. Use a bit of spray starch to give the embroidery a crisp feel.

Assembling the Wall Hanging

Press all seam allowances as indicated by the arrows.

1 Trim the finished embroidery to measure 4½" × 7½", keeping the design centered.

2 Sew the ¾" × 7½" dark blue rectangles to the left and right sides of the embroidered rectangle. Sew the ¾" × 5" dark blue rectangles to the top and bottom of the unit.

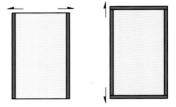

3 Sew the 1½" × 8" blue #1 rectangle to the left edge of the unit and the 1½" × 8" blue #2 rectangle to the right edge.

4 Stitch the 1½" × 7" dark blue rectangle to the top of the assembled unit and the 1½" × 7" blue-dot rectangle to the bottom edge of the unit.

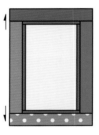

5 Add the 1" × 7" rectangles of dark blue print, blue #2, and blue #1 to the bottom edge of the unit in order.

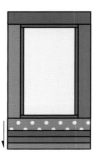

Buttonhole Loops

If you wish to display your hanging on a wire frame like the one shown, make buttonhole-stitch loops on the back of the project to slip over the wire support.

Buttonhole stitch is worked like blanket stitch, but the stitches are positioned close together. To begin, bring the needle to the right side of the fabric at 1. Insert the needle at point 2, above and to the right of point 1, and rock the needle to bring it out again at point 3. Be sure the working thread passes under the point of the needle at 3. Pull the needle through the fabric and tighten the stitch. Point 3 becomes point 1 for the next stitch.

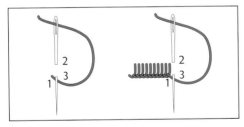

Buttonhole stitch

For these loops, the buttonhole stitches will be worked around foundation stitches and the needle will only enter the fabric at the beginning and end of each loop. Decide where the loops will be placed to hold the work correctly on your frame and mark four locations evenly spaced across the backing. For the featured quilt, the loops begin 1" below the top edge of the hanging.

1 Take three or four straight stitches at the first mark with pearl cotton, making the stitches ⅜" long and placing them close together. Sew through the backing fabric *only* so that the stitches aren't visible from the front of the project.

Mark the backing.

2 Bring the needle to the right side of the fabric at one end of the foundation stitches. Work buttonhole stitches over the straight stitches, placing the buttonhole stitches close together to cover the base threads. Cover the entire length of the base stitches, and then draw the needle back into the backing fabric. Secure the thread end, bury the thread tail, and clip the tail close to the fabric. Repeat to make three more loops.

If you prefer a different display method, you may want to attach a hanging sleeve to the backing, or attach ribbon loops to the top edge of the wall hanging.

Finishing the Quilt

For help with the following finishing steps, go to ShopMartingale.com/HowtoQuilt for free, illustrated instructions.

1 Layer and baste the quilt top, batting, and 7" × 11½" blue print #1 backing rectangle. Quilt by hand or machine. The quilt shown is quilted using ecru pearl cotton and a running stitch ⅛" above each of the three lowest seamlines. The embroidered rectangle is stitched ⅛" inside the perimeter seams.

2 Make buttonhole loops for hanging (see page 239).

3 Using the blue tone-on-tone 2"-wide strip, prepare and attach double-fold binding.

4 Optional: attach a snowman button to the lower portion of the hanging as shown in the quilt photo.

Satin stitch

Straight stitch

Bead

French knot
(2 wraps)

I'm A Little Snowman
Short and Fat
Here is my Broomstick
Here is my Hat!

French knot
(2 wraps)

Embroidery Key

——— Backstitch

– – – Running stitch

■ Satin stitch

• French knot

— Straight stitch

✕✕ Cross-stitch